USBORNE BATTLEGAME
KNIGHTS AT WAR

ANDREW McNEIL

Acknowledgements
We wish to thank the following individuals and organizations for their assistance and for making available material in their collections.

A. F. Kersting
Mary Evans Picture Library
The Mansell Collection
The Tower of London

Illustrators
Roland Berry
Gerry Embleton
John Hutchinson
Angus McBride
Michael Roffe
Brian Watson

Art and editorial direction
David Jefferis
Rules editor
James Opie
Text editors
Tony Allan
Margaret Chester
Picture researcher
Caroline Lucas

First published in 1975 by Usborne Publishing Ltd, Usborne House, 83-85 Saffron Hill, London EC1N 8RT, England.

This edition first published in 1991.

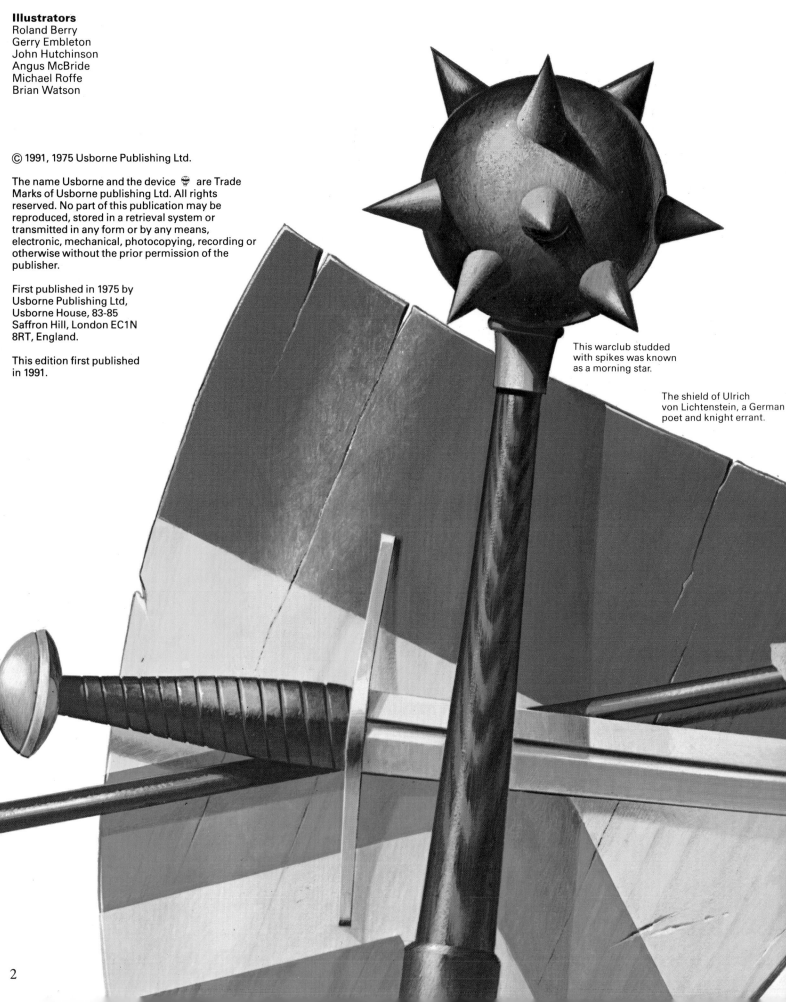

This warclub studded with spikes was known as a morning star.

The shield of Ulrich von Lichtenstein, a German poet and knight errant.

ABOUT THIS BOOK

Knights at War tells the violent story of the mounted warriors of the Middle Ages. It includes four games, complete with rules, pull-out boards and cut-out pieces, that let you relive the epic struggles of the age of the sword.

The book paints a vivid picture of the days when a horse, a suit of armour and enough skill to use them well could make a man almost unbeatable on the battlefield. It tells of the rough-and-tumble world of tournaments. How castles were besieged. What made the crusaders go to fight in the searing heat of the Holy Land.

The games are based on real combat situations. In 'Border Raiders', knights try to drive back invaders who are burning villages and plundering cattle. 'Tournament' recreates the thrills and spills of jousting. In 'Siege!' rival lords struggle for control of a castle; and you can fight out Richard Lionheart's decisive battle against Saladin at Arsouf.

CONTENTS

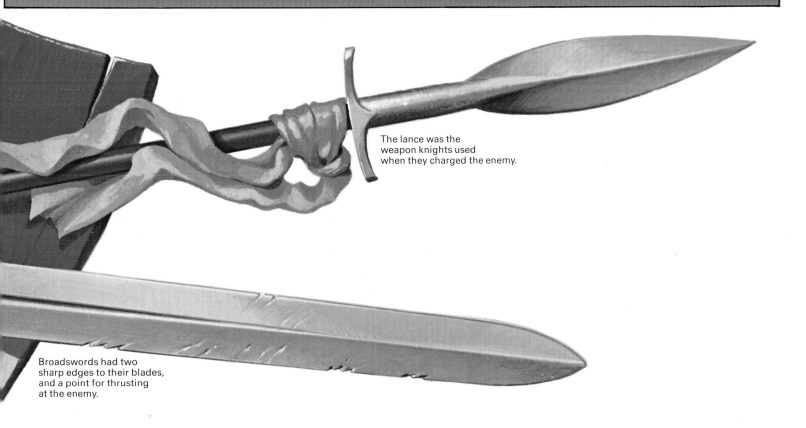

The lance was the weapon knights used when they charged the enemy.

Broadswords had two sharp edges to their blades, and a point for thrusting at the enemy.

3

WARRIORS ON HORSEBACK

The knights of the Middle Ages were soldiers who fought on horseback. The French word for a knight, *chevalier*, simply means horseman. In German the word is *ritter*, or rider.

Knights played the most important part in warfare during the Middle Ages, from about A.D. 900 to 1500. This was because in those days soldiers on horses, or cavalry, could always beat those on foot. Later, foot-soldiers learnt to stand up to cavalry charges. Knights then became less important.

Early horse soldiers
A soldier on horseback uses the weight and speed of his horse to charge the enemy. The Romans had cavalry but they did not usually charge. Their soldiers wore heavy armour, and their horses were too small and light to carry so much weight in a charge. The Romans won their battles with well-trained foot-soldiers.

The first real knights appeared in France, in about 800. Four hundred years before that, the Western Roman Empire had been defeated and overrun by tribes from the north and east. One of these tribes, from what is now northern Germany, was the Franks. They were very fierce and clever fighters. Under their leader, Clovis, they defeated the other tribes. By the year 500 they had conquered the whole of what is now France.

Over the next 300 years the Franks held their lands successfully against many enemies and also won more. By 800 a large part of Germany and Italy, as well as France, belonged to them. Their leader, Charlemagne, was crowned Emperor by the Pope in Rome in 800. His lands became known as the Holy Roman Empire. It was in the reign of Charlemagne that knights first became important.

Over the years the Franks had used horses more and more in battle. They had discovered the use of the stirrup. The soldier was now held firmly in the saddle, and could throw his whole weight, and that of his horse, behind his lance. Bigger and stronger horses had been bred since Roman times, so that more armour could be worn. By Charlemagne's time it was difficult to stand up to soldiers charging on horseback.

The feudal system
But only a rich man could keep horses and get armour for battle. The king or emperor needed properly armed horsemen to fight for him against his enemies. So he gave land to his closest followers. In return they promised to fight for him themselves and to bring their followers with them.

A nobleman would give land in the same way to his closest followers and would see that they had horses, armour and weapons. In return these horsemen, or knights, would promise to fight under their lord for the king. They too had followers to whom they gave land or food and shelter in return for service. This is what is called feudalism – a way of government that soon spread all over Europe.

Norman conquests
The most successful knights were the Normans. They lived in a part of France that had been given to their ancestors, the Norsemen, by the King of France in 911. The Norsemen were sailors, but in Normandy they soon learnt to fight on horseback and became very skilful knights.

At the Battle of Hastings, in 1066, the Normans proved clearly that the foot-soldier of the time could not hope to defeat a mounted knight. The Anglo-Saxons, under Harold, fought on foot with long axes and big shields. The Normans defeated them by cavalry charges, backed up by archery.

The Normans not only conquered England. They also spread further into France, and won land in Sicily and southern Italy. They even attacked the mighty Byzantine empire in its Greek homeland. The impact of their cavalry charges was so great that a small group of Norman knights could often defeat a whole army.

Byrnie and hauberk
The Norman knights who won the Battle of Hastings wore shirts of mail, called byrnies. The word mail comes from the French and means net. The byrnie was made of metal rings linked together over a leather shirt. It was long enough to cover the horseman's knees, to protect him from foot-soldiers' swords or axes.

To protect his neck the knight wore a tight-fitting hood of mail, called a hauberk. Later the byrnie and hauberk were joined together. Over the hauberk the knight wore a cone-shaped helmet with a nose-piece. He fought with a sword and lance, and carried a kite-shaped shield.

At the time of the Normans all the knights of western Europe were armed in much the same way. And they all held their land under the feudal system.

Rulers and rebels
The lords for whom they fought were vassals, or servants, of the sovereign lord – the king or emperor. But the vassals often became very powerful. Sometimes vassals became more powerful than their sovereign and rebelled against him. So there was always fighting for the knights to do, either for the sovereign or against him.

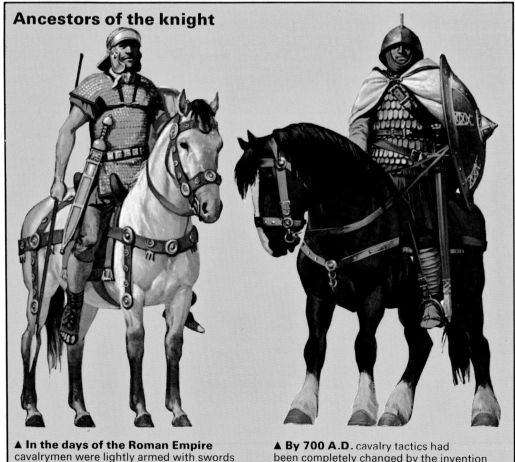

Ancestors of the knight

▲ **In the days of the Roman Empire** cavalrymen were lightly armed with swords and throwing spears, and they rode small, nimble horses. They often had to dismount to fight on foot, and their weapons and armour were virtually the same as those borne by the infantry.

▲ **By 700 A.D.** cavalry tactics had been completely changed by the invention of the stirrup. Horse soldiers were securely seated, and could charge the enemy with lances. The Franks rode heavy horses crossbred from French and Caucasian strains for increased stamina.

▶ **Much of what we know** about the Normans comes from the Bayeux Tapestry. This 73m-long (240ft) embroidery describes the invasion of England in strip-cartoon style.

The Normans expand their empire, A.D. 1066

The Normans were originally Norsemen, Viking pirates who raided and eventually settled in what is now Normandy in northern France. There they learned to speak French and were converted to Christianity. Their kingdom was the best governed in Europe.

They were also Europe's finest fighting men. They became skilled riders. Their mailed horsemen swept all opposition before them. Eager to win new lands, the Normans gladly agreed to follow their Duke, William, when he proposed an attack on England.

They met the army of the Anglo-Saxon King Harold near Hastings. Harold's men took their stand on a hill. The Norman archers attacked first, firing volleys of arrows upwards to fall on the enemy from above. But the foot-soldiers stood firm.

Even the Norman cavalry failed at first to break through. But by nightfall repeated charges had worn down the Anglo-Saxon ranks. When King Harold himself was killed, the last resistance crumbled. The Norman knights had won themselves a new kingdom.

FIGHT FOR THE HOLY LAND

The Crusades were wars waged by the Christian kings and knights of western Europe against the Moslem rulers of Palestine.

Jerusalem had been in the hands of the Moslems since 638. But Christian pilgrims had always been allowed to visit the Holy Places there. Then in 1071 the Seljuk Turks conquered Palestine. They treated the Christians badly. So the Byzantine Emperor appealed to the rulers of western Europe for help in protecting the Christians.

Christians of the east

Byzantium, or Constantinople, was the capital of the eastern Roman Empire. When the old Roman Empire was overrun by the barbarian tribes, the eastern part survived. Its rulers had many eastern customs. But they were Christians.

The Byzantines had fought bravely against the Turks for many years. But they had been badly defeated at Manzikert in 1071 and they now had to turn to the west for help.

The knights of Europe were quite willing to go to their aid. They did not specially want to fight for the Emperor. But they did want to save the Holy Places.

The First Crusade

The First Crusade began in 1096. Thousands of knights, in many different groups and by various routes, made the difficult journey to Constantinople. From there they marched into Asia Minor and the lands recently won by the Turks.

The Turks soon found that they could not stand up to the crusaders' charges in open battle. So they took refuge in their cities. These the crusaders attacked and captured one by one by siege. Jerusalem itself fell in July, 1099.

The leaders of the First Crusade set up four states, Jerusalem, Antioch, Edessa and Tripoli. All the states were governed by the feudal system. Large castles were built and more and more knights came from Europe to defend them. But under skilful leaders the Moslems won back the four big cities in turn – Edessa in 1144, Jerusalem in 1187, Antioch in 1268, and Tripoli in 1289.

Richard and Saladin

After each Moslem victory a new crusade was organized and more western knights went to the east to fight. The best-known Crusade is the Third, in which Richard the Lionheart of England fought against Saladin. This began after Saladin had won back Jerusalem in 1187.

The western knights fought well. But Saladin was a brilliant general and did not let them use their charge against his mounted bowmen. So the crusaders failed to recapture the city.

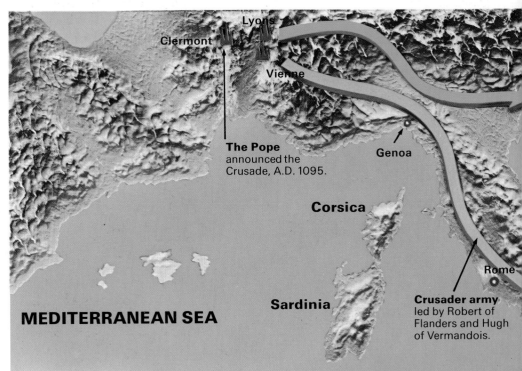

The western knights wanted to keep an army in Palestine to protect the Holy Places. For this, religious orders of knighthood were set up. The members of the orders were like fighting monks. They did not marry or own any possessions. They could spend their whole lives fighting the Moslems.

There were three great military orders: the Hospitallers, the Templars and the Teutonic (German) Knights. Their members fought with superb discipline. Many battles against the Moslems were lost because other knights charged the enemy too soon. The knights of the military orders always stood firm and fought bravely to the last man.

Loss of the Holy Land

The Moslems won back the last of their possessions in Palestine at the end of the 13th century, and the military orders had to leave. The Hospitallers went to the island of Rhodes. The Templars did not survive for long. They were attacked by the King of France and later by other rulers of Europe. Their vast wealth was taken from them and their leaders were killed.

The Teutonic Knights went to eastern Germany and started a crusade against people who were still not Christians. From their great fortress at Marienburg in Poland they created a vast new state.

Effects of the Crusades

The Crusades were very important in the development of knighthood. They gave the knights of western Europe a chance to fight, and to win new lands and riches.

They also taught the western knights how they should behave. Men like King Richard the Lionheart, St Louis of France, Hermann von Salza and Godfrey of Bouillon devoted their lives to crusading. The knights admired them and brought up their sons to be like them.

▲ **In 1095 Pope Urban II** summoned a council of the Church at Clermont in the south of France. He appealed to all knights to aid the Christians of the east and to free Jerusalem. The knights were to wear a cross on their clothes; from the Latin word for this they took the name 'crusader'.

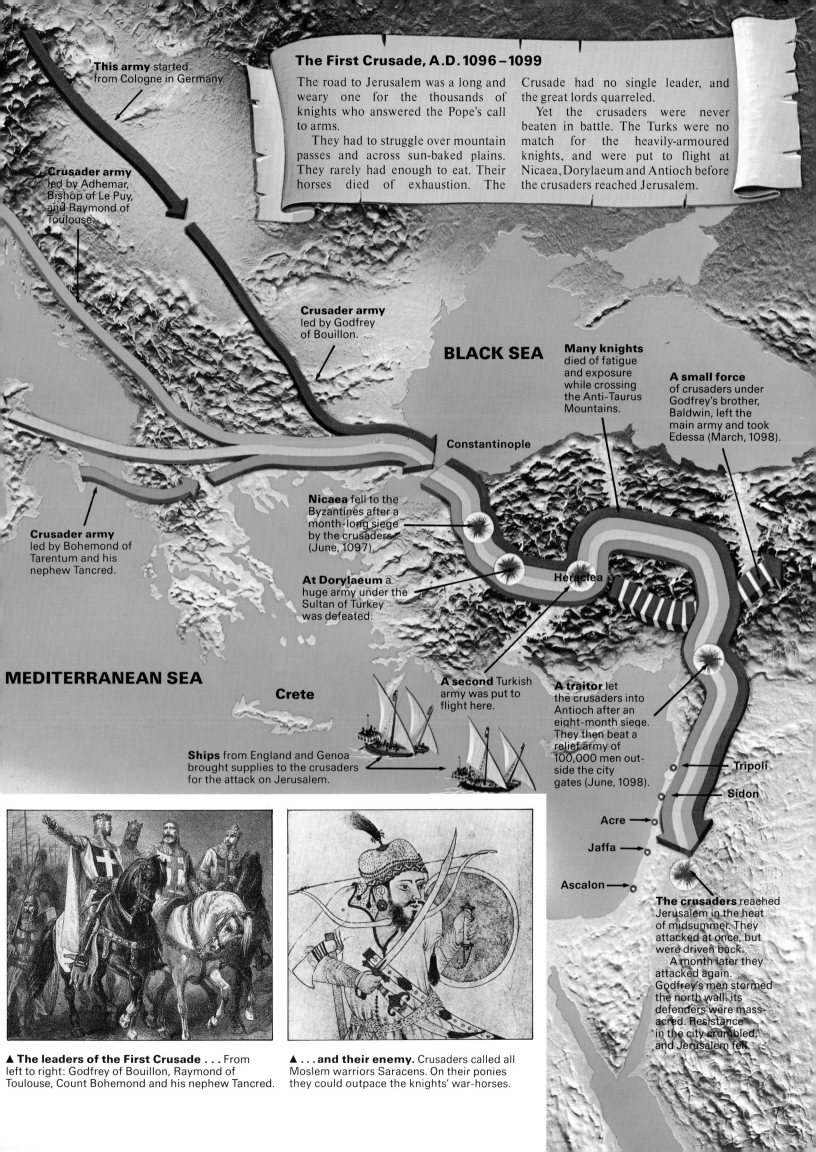

This army started from Cologne in Germany.

Crusader army led by Adhemar, Bishop of Le Puy, and Raymond of Toulouse.

The First Crusade, A.D. 1096–1099

The road to Jerusalem was a long and weary one for the thousands of knights who answered the Pope's call to arms.

They had to struggle over mountain passes and across sun-baked plains. They rarely had enough to eat. Their horses died of exhaustion. The Crusade had no single leader, and the great lords quarreled.

Yet the crusaders were never beaten in battle. The Turks were no match for the heavily-armoured knights, and were put to flight at Nicaea, Dorylaeum and Antioch before the crusaders reached Jerusalem.

Crusader army led by Godfrey of Bouillon.

BLACK SEA

Many knights died of fatigue and exposure while crossing the Anti-Taurus Mountains.

A small force of crusaders under Godfrey's brother, Baldwin, left the main army and took Edessa (March, 1098).

Constantinople

Nicaea fell to the Byzantines after a month-long siege by the crusaders (June, 1097).

Crusader army led by Bohemond of Tarentum and his nephew Tancred.

At Dorylaeum a huge army under the Sultan of Turkey was defeated.

Heraclea

MEDITERRANEAN SEA

Crete

A second Turkish army was put to flight here.

A traitor let the crusaders into Antioch after an eight-month siege. They then beat a relief army of 100,000 men outside the city gates (June, 1098).

Ships from England and Genoa brought supplies to the crusaders for the attack on Jerusalem.

Tripoli

Sidon

Acre

Jaffa

Ascalon

The crusaders reached Jerusalem in the heat of midsummer. They attacked at once, but were driven back.
A month later they attacked again. Godfrey's men stormed the north wall. Its defenders were massacred. Resistance in the city crumbled, and Jerusalem fell.

▲ **The leaders of the First Crusade . . .** From left to right: Godfrey of Bouillon, Raymond of Toulouse, Count Bohemond and his nephew Tancred.

▲ **. . . and their enemy.** Crusaders called all Moslem warriors Saracens. On their ponies they could outpace the knights' war-horses.

7

STRONGHOLDS OF THE KNIGHTS

Every lord needed a castle to protect his lands. Castles were not just places to live in. They usually guarded roads, valleys or river crossings. No raider would dare to come too near a castle, with its strong walls, reserves of men and stores of food and arms.

Norman castles

The Franks at first used wooden towers to defend their lands against the Norsemen. The Normans made these stronger by placing them on artificial mounds, called 'mottes'. There was a larger area below, where stores and cattle could be kept. This was called the bailey, meaning 'safe area'. Bailey and tower would be surrounded by a wooden palisade, or fence, and a ditch.

The Normans could build this sort of castle very quickly. They built hundreds of them in England and the other countries they conquered. In time they rebuilt the wooden towers in stone.

Once stone was used, the towers could be made much higher, and the walls thicker. The living-rooms became more comfortable. The old wooden palisade might be rebuilt in stone. These stone castles took a long time to build and cost a lot of money.

When the knights of Europe went to the east for the First Crusade, they were amazed at the size and strength of the castles they saw. A castle must be as strong as the methods used to attack it. The Byzantines and Turks had much better siege engines than those used in western Europe.

In the east the knights learnt to build strong outer walls for their castles and to protect the walls with flanking towers. The central tower – called the keep, or donjon – became less important. All the parts of the castle fitted together to make a strong defence.

The knights also learnt to build round towers instead of square ones. They were not so easy to undermine. Spiral staircases were built, to protect the defender's body but leave the attacker exposed. In dark places steep steps or holes were hidden, down which an enemy could fall. There were secret places, too, for keeping prisoners until they were ransomed.

Strengthening the defences

Next came the 'concentric' castle. This had two sets of walls, both with flanking towers. If an enemy was clever enough to get through one set of walls, he could still be defeated at the second.

Gateways became specially important. In the older castles they had been the weakest spot. A special set of walls and towers was built to protect the gate. This was called the barbican. It made the gateway very strong, especially if it had a drawbridge and portcullis too.

Thousands of castles were built all over Europe. The strongest were put in places where there was always a danger of raids. King Edward I of England built a chain of castles on the Welsh border, among them Harlech, Beaumaris and Caernarvon. The Teutonic Knights constructed large fortresses, such as Thorn and Marienburg, to protect the lands they conquered in eastern Europe.

Krak des Chevaliers

The most magnificent castle of all was Krak des Chevaliers. This was built by the Hospitallers in Palestine. It took 30 years to build. Krak had a beautiful chapel and great wall, and enormous cellars for the stores needed by large numbers of men during a siege. Saladin failed to capture it, but it finally fell to the Turks in 1271.

Castles stopped being built when armies began to use cannon. They cost too much for most lords to keep up. When new and properly looked after and manned they were difficult to take, except by a trick or treachery, or after a long siege. But often they began to decay soon after they were built, and then they were easy to take.

300 years of castle design

▼ **The Normans built** motte-and-bailey castles that could be constructed quickly to provide shelter for their men in newly-conquered lands. The weakness of castles of this type was that their wooden defences could easily be set on fire.

▼ **Stronger castles of stone** were built in the 1100s. Their main feature was the huge square tower called the donjon. These castles were often built by barons who used them as private strongholds to increase their power.

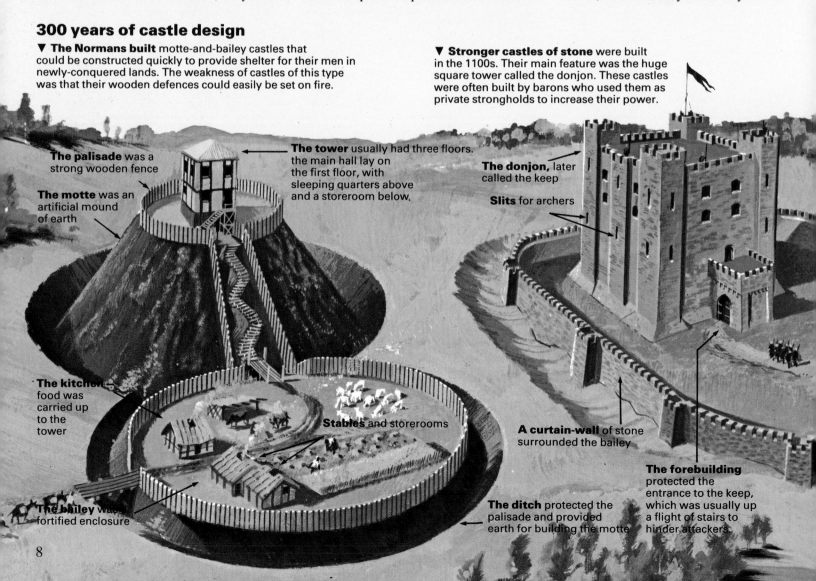

The palisade was a strong wooden fence

The motte was an artificial mound of earth

The tower usually had three floors. the main hall lay on the first floor, with sleeping quarters above and a storeroom below.

The donjon, later called the keep

Slits for archers

The kitchen food was carried up to the tower

Stables and storerooms

A curtain-wall of stone surrounded the bailey

The bailey was a fortified enclosure

The ditch protected the palisade and provided earth for building the motte

The forebuilding protected the entrance to the keep, which was usually up a flight of stairs to hinder attackers.

▲ **The crusaders built castles** throughout the lands they conquered. Krak des Chevaliers (arrowed) lies in what is now Syria.

MEDITERRANEAN SEA

Jerusalem

The finest castle of them all

Krak des Chevaliers – the Knight's Castle – was the largest and strongest of all the crusader castles. It lies on a hilltop 760m (2,500ft) up in the Syrian highlands. At the time of the Crusades it could hold 2,000 men, and later a whole village grew up within its walls. The Hospitallers held it against Saladin. It was besieged again in 1271, when the lack of food forced the garrison to surrender in return for a safe conduct to the coast.

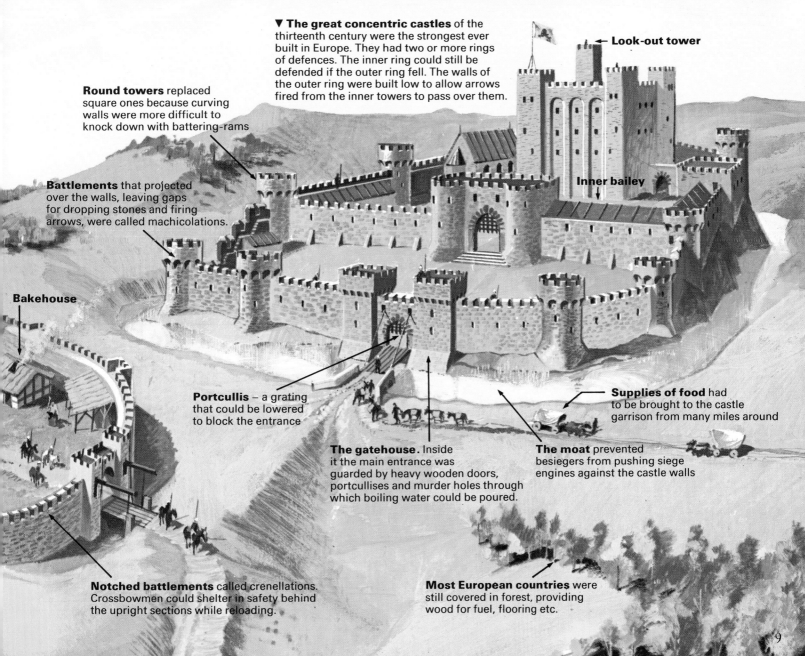

▼ **The great concentric castles** of the thirteenth century were the strongest ever built in Europe. They had two or more rings of defences. The inner ring could still be defended if the outer ring fell. The walls of the outer ring were built low to allow arrows fired from the inner towers to pass over them.

← **Look-out tower**

Round towers replaced square ones because curving walls were more difficult to knock down with battering-rams

Battlements that projected over the walls, leaving gaps for dropping stones and firing arrows, were called machicolations.

Inner bailey

Bakehouse

Portcullis – a grating that could be lowered to block the entrance

Supplies of food had to be brought to the castle garrison from many miles around

The gatehouse. Inside it the main entrance was guarded by heavy wooden doors, portcullises and murder holes through which boiling water could be poured.

The moat prevented besiegers from pushing siege engines against the castle walls

Notched battlements called crenellations. Crossbowmen could shelter in safety behind the upright sections while reloading.

Most European countries were still covered in forest, providing wood for fuel, flooring etc.

DRESSING FOR BATTLE

A knight wore armour to ward off the arrows and sword-thrusts of the enemy, especially in the charge.

Knights who fought at Hastings and in the First Crusade wore mail armour and cone-shaped helmets with nose-pieces. This armour protected most of the body against arrows fired from the short bows then used. It also warded off sword-blows quite well. It was not so useful against a well-aimed lance or a heavy weapon like an axe or mace.

Helms and helmets

The first part of the armour to be improved was the head-covering. Early helmets had been made of hard leather or pieces of metal. Then the helmets were made from one piece of metal. The Normans added a metal piece to their helmets to protect the neck. Later the helmet was made to cover the whole head. It had narrow slits for the knight to see through. This type was called a helm.

The earliest helms were flat on top. This meant that they could be cut open with axes and maces in close fighting after the charge. A blow was more likely to glance off a point, or a cone. So the pointed casque, or basinet was made, with hinged pieces coming down over the face (visors). These were widely used in battle.

Armour made to measure

In the 1300s, as armourers became more skilled, more and more plate-armour was used. This was made from sheets of metal. It was stronger than mail, without being heavier. And it could be shaped so that blows would glance off it.

Legs and arms were the first parts to be covered with plate-armour. Extra care had to be taken with the covering of elbows and knees, so that the wearer could move about easily. The armour, known as 'harness', had to be made specially for the wearer if it was to fit properly.

Knights still wore mail under the plate-armour. Only rich men could afford a whole armour of plate. Under the mail they wore a thick padded tunic. All these layers protected the knight, but they made fighting a hot and tiring business.

Fighting on horseback

A knight could move about quite easily in armour. But he was in great danger if he fell off his horse. The fall often stunned or injured him. He could be killed or captured by foot-soldiers if he did not get up quickly. So archers and other foot-soldiers aimed at the knight's horse to bring him down.

Some knights tried to protect their horses with armour. But only a few could afford mail or plate-armour. Leather was sometimes used, but most horses went into battle almost unprotected.

During the 1400s mail stopped being made and only plate-armour was used. Earlier some parts of the body, like the loins and neck, could only be covered by mail. But now armourers had learnt to make plate-armour for them too.

A better head-covering, called the armet, was made, with the good points of both helm and basinet. It rested on the shoulders instead of the head, and so was more comfortable.

In the 1100s a knight wore a coat over his armour. On it were his armorial bearings – a sort of badge to show who he was. At first the coat was long, coming below the knee. This got in the knight's way, and it became shorter until it disappeared. But the knight's armorial bearings continued to be called his coat of arms.

Sword, shield and lance

Every knight had a sword and small dagger hung on a belt. He also carried a lance and shield, and wore spurs.

A knight had to be very strong to fight with very heavy weapons in armour. He was taught as a child to ride a horse well, and trained to use lance and sword properly. With this training the knights won victories in Europe and the east for 400 years.

▶ **Fighting was a costly business** for this German knight. He wears several layers of expensive protective clothing. His suit of mail is reinforced with plate armour at the points where it is most likely to be struck in battle.

Roundels of plate metal protected the shoulder and elbow

The shield was made of wood or leather, not metal, and was decorated with the knight's coat of arms. He fitted it over his shoulder with a strap called a guige.

The great helm was put on at the last moment before battle. The knight's shoulders bore its weight.

This knight wears leather gloves, though iron gauntlets were also used.

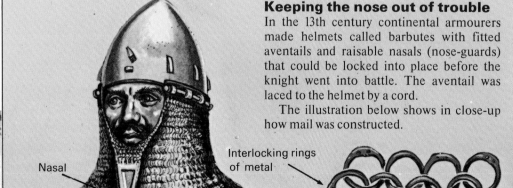

Keeping the nose out of trouble
In the 13th century continental armourers made helmets called barbutes with fitted aventails and raisable nasals (nose-guards) that could be locked into place before the knight went into battle. The aventail was laced to the helmet by a cord.

The illustration below shows in close-up how mail was constructed.

Nasal

Interlocking rings of metal

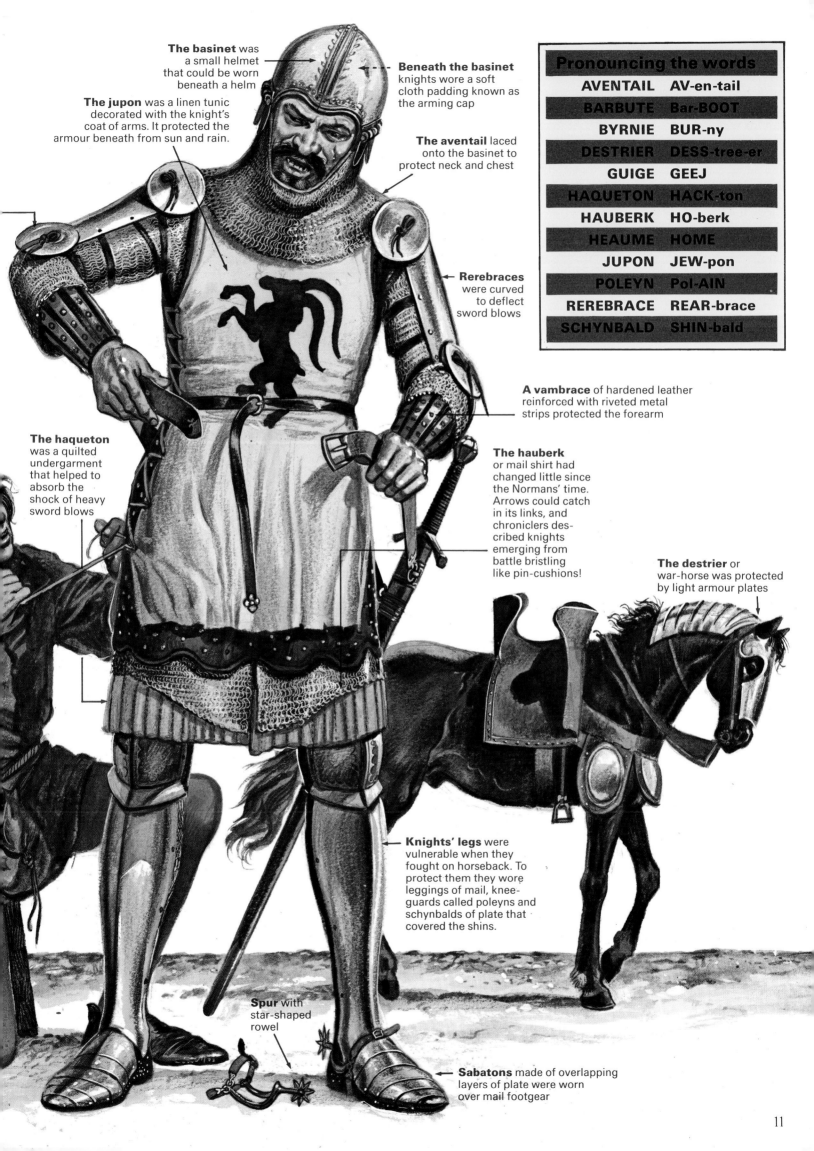

The basinet was a small helmet that could be worn beneath a helm

Beneath the basinet knights wore a soft cloth padding known as the arming cap

The jupon was a linen tunic decorated with the knight's coat of arms. It protected the armour beneath from sun and rain.

The aventail laced onto the basinet to protect neck and chest

Rerebraces were curved to deflect sword blows

The haqueton was a quilted undergarment that helped to absorb the shock of heavy sword blows

A vambrace of hardened leather reinforced with riveted metal strips protected the forearm

The hauberk or mail shirt had changed little since the Normans' time. Arrows could catch in its links, and chroniclers described knights emerging from battle bristling like pin-cushions!

The destrier or war-horse was protected by light armour plates

Knights' legs were vulnerable when they fought on horseback. To protect them they wore leggings of mail, knee-guards called poleyns and schynbalds of plate that covered the shins.

Spur with star-shaped rowel

Sabatons made of overlapping layers of plate were worn over mail footgear

Pronouncing the words	
AVENTAIL	AV-en-tail
BARBUTE	Bar-BOOT
BYRNIE	BUR-ny
DESTRIER	DESS-tree-er
GUIGE	GEEJ
HAQUETON	HACK-ton
HAUBERK	HO-berk
HEAUME	HOME
JUPON	JEW-pon
POLEYN	Pol-AIN
REREBRACE	REAR-brace
SCHYNBALD	SHIN-bald

HERALDRY

Early knights sometimes decorated their shields with colours and patterns. At first these had no special meaning. Then, during the 1100s, knights began to put what are called armorial bearings, or 'arms', on their shields.

Sign-language of war

A knight's arms were a sort of label, showing by signs and pictures who he was. These labels were needed in battle, when a knight's face was hidden by his helmet. But they were no use if they could not be understood, or if two knights wore the same label. So very strict rules were made, deciding what each sign and picture was to mean, and who was allowed to wear it.

Like most things to do with knights, the rules came from France, and all the parts of the arms, and their colours, were named in old French.

The people who made the rules, and saw that they were kept, were the heralds. It was they who carried messages and gave signals in battle, and counted the dead afterwards. So they had to know who everyone was. The study of arms and the rules about them is called heraldry.

The heralds decided who had the right to wear arms and what signs each knight could put on them. Some designs were so popular that there were quarrels over them, which the heralds had to settle.

From father to son

A knight who had had his arms approved by the heralds could pass them on to his son. The son might then want to add more signs, describing himself or perhaps showing who his mother was. So as they were passed down the arms often became more complicated, with several small pictures on them instead of one big one.

At first arms were very simple. There might be a cross, to show that the knight was a crusader, or a lion, to show that he was brave. So many knights wanted these signs that the heralds had to invent all sorts of different crosses. Lions were drawn in different positions – lying down (couchant), or on their hind-legs (rampant).

Crusading knights sometimes put *bougets* – skins for carrying water – in their arms. Pieces of armour were shown, such as spurs or links of mail. Sometimes there were household objects, for instance spindles or the fashionable long sleeves called manches.

Every part of the shield was given a name. This made it easy for heralds and knights to describe shields. They always started with the main colour, called the field. Then they described how it was divided and what was on the divisions.

Colours for combat

The colours used were those that were easiest to make. Red and blue were more common than green. Light colours were put next to dark ones, so that they all stood out well.

The two light colours used were yellow and white. They were called metals, after gold and silver. The other colours were called tinctures. The small circles, or roundels, used in the designs were given different names depending on their colours. A gold roundel was called a bezant because it looked like a Byzantine coin of that name.

At first knights put their arms on their shields. This is why arms are shown shaped like shields. Later they were put on the coats the knights wore over their armour, and also on their banners and horses. The knight's followers wore their master's arms on their coats.

Knights also wore crests on top of their helmets to show who they were. These were made of boiled leather or wood, and were in the shape of heraldic signs. When men-at-arms began to wear armour too, knights could often be recognized from a distance by their crests.

Badges, mottoes and banners

Most knights also had badges. Sometimes these showed a part of the whole arms. Badges were often worn by servants instead of the whole arms, especially when the arms had become complicated, with a lot of divisions.

The knight would also have a motto, a sort of battle-cry or a word or sentence that he liked.

When knights could do without shields in battle, because their armour was so strong, they could be recognized by their banners. These were long, narrow flags. On them were the knight's badges, mottoes and arms.

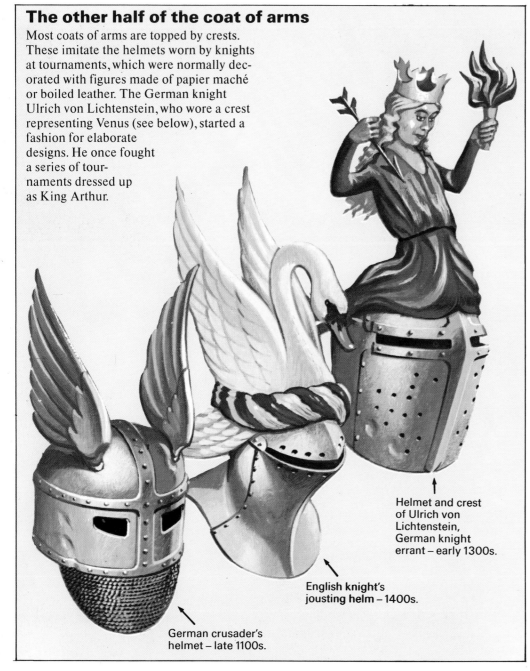

The other half of the coat of arms

Most coats of arms are topped by crests. These imitate the helmets worn by knights at tournaments, which were normally decorated with figures made of papier maché or boiled leather. The German knight Ulrich von Lichtenstein, who wore a crest representing Venus (see below), started a fashion for elaborate designs. He once fought a series of tournaments dressed up as King Arthur.

Helmet and crest of Ulrich von Lichtenstein, German knight errant – early 1300s.

English knight's jousting helm – 1400s.

German crusader's helmet – late 1100s.

The language of heraldry

The heralds developed a language of their own to describe the designs on knights' shields. It is still used for coats of arms today. Gold and silver are called metals. Like the other colours, metals have special heraldic names.

The form a design takes – for example the way it splits in half – is its division. Basic patterns are known as ordinaries. Coats of arms may also bear picture symbols called charges. Special terms are used for the two sides of the shield. Dexter means on the wearer's right, and sinister refers to the left hand side.

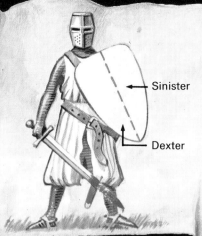

Sinister

Dexter

The colours of heraldry

Metals

Or (gold)   Argent (silver)   Sable (black)

Gules (red)   Azure (blue)   Vert (green)   Purpure (purple)

Divisions and ordinaries

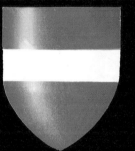

A fesse crosses the shield sideways

A vertical bar is called a pale

This Y-shaped pattern is a pall

A chevron

A wavy division is an ordée

This shield is divided quarterly

A bend

A saltire, or St Andrew's cross

A Greek cross

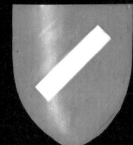

The sign of illegitimacy – a baton sinister

Charges – animals, weapons and flowers

A lion rampant

A walking lion is described as passant

A fabulous creature – the unicorn

A dragon

A double-headed eagle

The clenched fist

The scimitar shows an eastern influence

The battle axe was a popular charge

The fleur-de-lys of France

The red rose of Lancaster, England

DOWNFALL OF THE KNIGHTS

Knights were always victorious in battle until their enemies learnt to stand up to their charge. Even then they could still have won battles if they had changed their way of fighting. But they would not learn from their mistakes. They were beaten again and again and in the end disappeared from the battlefield.

The foot-soldier's revenge

Three weapons could defeat the knight if they were properly used: the longbow, the pike and the gun. They were all weapons of the foot-soldier.

The longbow was the weapon of the English. It was much more powerful than the short bow used by the Byzantines and the Turks. At Crécy, in 1346, the English longbowmen massacred the knights of France. They did the same at Poitiers, in 1356. The French failed to learn their lesson and were beaten again in 1415 at Agincourt.

In time the French learnt to stop the English using their archers. They used cannon to beat the English at Formigny in 1450 and at Castillon in 1453. The French made the best use of these primitive early cannon.

Victories of the pikemen

The pike was the weapon of the Scots and the Swiss. At Bannockburn in 1314 the Scots defeated an English force that included 2,000 knights. The Swiss made even better use of the pike in warfare against knights. They did this by using the halberd too. The long pikes stopped the knights' charge. The halberd, a cross between an axe and a spear, was used for killing at close quarters.

The Swiss showed the other countries of Europe that knights could be beaten by foot-soldiers. It was much cheaper to equip a foot-soldier than a knight or a man-at-arms. Large armies could be formed from ordinary people.

Zizka's peasant army

Another answer to the knights' charge was found in the 1400s in Bohemia, in central Europe. Jan Zizka, the brilliant leader of a peasant army, put most of his men into large wagons. They were armed with primitive hand-guns, bows and flails. When the wagons were arranged in a circle the knights could not break through.

Zizka's Hussites, as the peasants were called, defeated every army sent against them. Later they mounted cannon on their wagons.

In the end the Hussites fought among themselves. Their tactics were only suited to the countries of central Europe. But they showed the rest of Europe how useful mobile cannon and hand-guns could be.

The knights still would not believe that they could be beaten by foot-soldiers. Over the years they had come to think that they were unbeatable. They looked down on foot-soldiers as peasants.

In fact knights did not always fight well. They would not always obey orders. They often threw themselves into battle without thinking, or worrying about tactics. As a result their battles were usually very bloody and large numbers of them were killed.

They also quarrelled and fought among themselves, in civil wars and feuds between families. Many nobles were wastefully killed in the English Wars of the Roses.

The end of knighthood

As the years went by the knights became less and less useful. As the feudal system disappeared they no longer had to fight for the king against his lords, or for higher nobles against other nobles.

Although the nobles and knights owned most of the land, the towns began to be important. Merchants in towns who wanted protection bought the services of foot-soldiers, or armoured horsemen who were not knights.

In the end the knights realized that foot-soldiers could beat them and they too began to fight on foot.

The rich nobles still supplied the cavalry of an army. But the infantry, or foot-soldiers, were now more useful. The knight in armour went on fighting in tournaments till the 1560s. But he disappeared from the battlefield.

What happened to the great orders of knighthood?

The Poor Knights of Christ and the Temple of Solomon

The Templars got their name because their headquarters was built on the site of Solomon's temple in Jerusalem. They were the first of the fighting orders, founded in 1118.

As their fame spread, kings and nobles granted them lands and castles. The Order became so wealthy that it aroused the envy of later rulers.

When the last crusaders were driven out of the Holy Land, the Order came under attack. In 1307 King Philip IV of France had all the Templars in his kingdom arrested and tortured. The Pope then ordered that the knights should go on trial. Though found not guilty in every country but France, they were condemned there. The Pope suppressed the Order, and the last Grand Master was burned at the stake.

The Knights of the Hospital of St John the Baptist

The Hospitallers rivalled the Templars both in their wealth and as soldiers, but through tactful leadership they made fewer enemies. After the loss of the Holy Land they moved their headquarters first to Cyprus and then to the Greek island of Rhodes. For 200 years they used this as a base for raids on Turkish ports and shipping. In 1522 they were forced to leave it after a siege by Sultan Suleiman the Magnificent.

They went to Malta, where they continued to be a thorn in the side of the Turks. Suleiman besieged them again in 1565. The knights put up a heroic resistance, and the Turks had to withdraw. The Hospitallers, by then usually known as the Knights of Malta, ultimately surrendered the island to Napoleon in 1798.

The Teutonic Knights

This Order was founded during the Fourth Crusade. It soon turned its attention from the Saracens to the pagan tribes of northern Europe, launching a full-scale crusade against the Prussians in 1230.

This was a strange and brutal war fought among marshes and pine forests. Captured knights were roasted alive in their armour as human sacrifices, and they in turn showed the enemy no mercy. Uniting with an existing order called the Brethren of the Sword, they carried the fight into Livonia, in what is now Russia. Despite some defeats, they managed to carve out a new state for themselves.

After a decisive defeat by the Polish army at Tannenberg in 1410, the Order went into decline. By 1550 their state had become a typical German duchy.

The Spanish Orders

For centuries before the Crusades began, Christians in Spain had been fighting the Moslem invaders who controlled much of their land. The Templars and Hospitallers were too busy in the Holy Land to fight in Spain, so Spanish knights banded together to drive the Moors out of Spain.

The Order of Calatrava was founded in 1158, and that of Santiago in 1175. The knights of Santiago, unlike those of other orders, were allowed to marry. The knights played an important part in the Battle of Las Navas de Tolosa against the Moors in 1212. When the reconquest was completed with the capture of Granada in 1492, there was no work left for the orders to do. The King of Spain took control of them, and they soon lost their importance.

PULL-OUT SECTION

The next ten pages include boards and cut-out
pieces for four battlegames. To remove them,
open the staples in the middle of the book and lift
out all these pages. Then close the staples to keep
the rest of the book intact.

Cut-out game pieces for the
'Battle of Arsouf' and **'Siege'**
are on the other side of this
page.

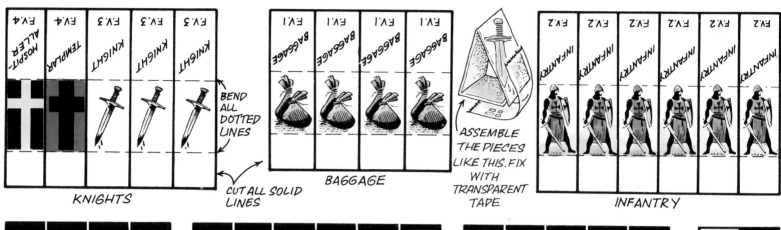

THE PIECES FOR ARSOUF

| HOSPIT-ALLER FV.4 | TEMPLAR FV.4 | KNIGHT FV.3 | KNIGHT FV.3 | KNIGHT FV.3 |

KNIGHTS

BEND ALL DOTTED LINES

CUT ALL SOLID LINES

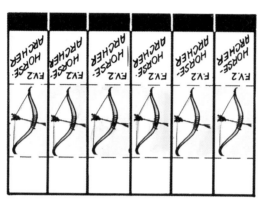

| BAGGAGE FV.1 | BAGGAGE FV.1 | BAGGAGE FV.1 | BAGGAGE FV.1 |

BAGGAGE

ASSEMBLE THE PIECES LIKE THIS. FIX WITH TRANSPARENT TAPE

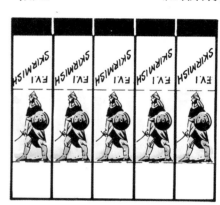

| INFANTRY FV.2 | INFANTRY FV.2 | INFANTRY FV.2 | INFANTRY FV.2 | INFANTRY FV.2 | INFANTRY FV.2 |

INFANTRY

| MAMELUKE FV.3 | MAMELUKE FV.3 | MAMELUKE FV.3 | MAMELUKE FV.3 |

MAMELUKES

| HORSE-ARCHER FV.2 | HORSE-ARCHER FV.2 | HORSE-ARCHER FV.2 | HORSE-ARCHER FV.2 | HORSE-ARCHER FV.2 |

HORSE-ARCHERS

| SKIRMISH FV.1 | SKIRMISH FV.1 | SKIRMISH FV.1 | SKIRMISH FV.1 | SKIRMISH FV.1 |

SKIRMISHERS

| RICHARD (+2) FV.2 | SALADIN (+2) FV.2 |

RICHARD SALADIN

THE PIECES FOR SIEGE!

THE ATTACKING ARMY

EARL D'ASSAULT

USE THIS SPINNER IF YOU DO NOT HAVE A DICE

THE DEFENDING ARMY

SPARE PIECES

HUGH DE FENDER

ROCKS

BOILING OIL

'GREEK FIRE'

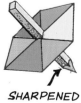

SHARPENED MATCHSTICK

The board for the **'Battle of Arsouf'** is on the other side. Remove it with the rest of the pull-out section by opening the staples in the middle of the book. You could use thin card to strengthen this board and make it last longer. Cut some card the same size as the board and then glue it to the plain side. You could also cover it with transparent, sticky-backed plastic.

ARSOUF

ROAD

THE BATTLE OF

ARSOUF

September 7, 1191

Stream

Moslem army starts
from here

The board for **'Siege'** is on the other side. Remove it with the rest of the pull-out section by opening the staples in the middle of the book. You could use thin card to strengthen this board and make it last longer. Cut some card the same size as the board and then glue it to the plain side. You could also cover it with transparent, sticky-backed plastic.

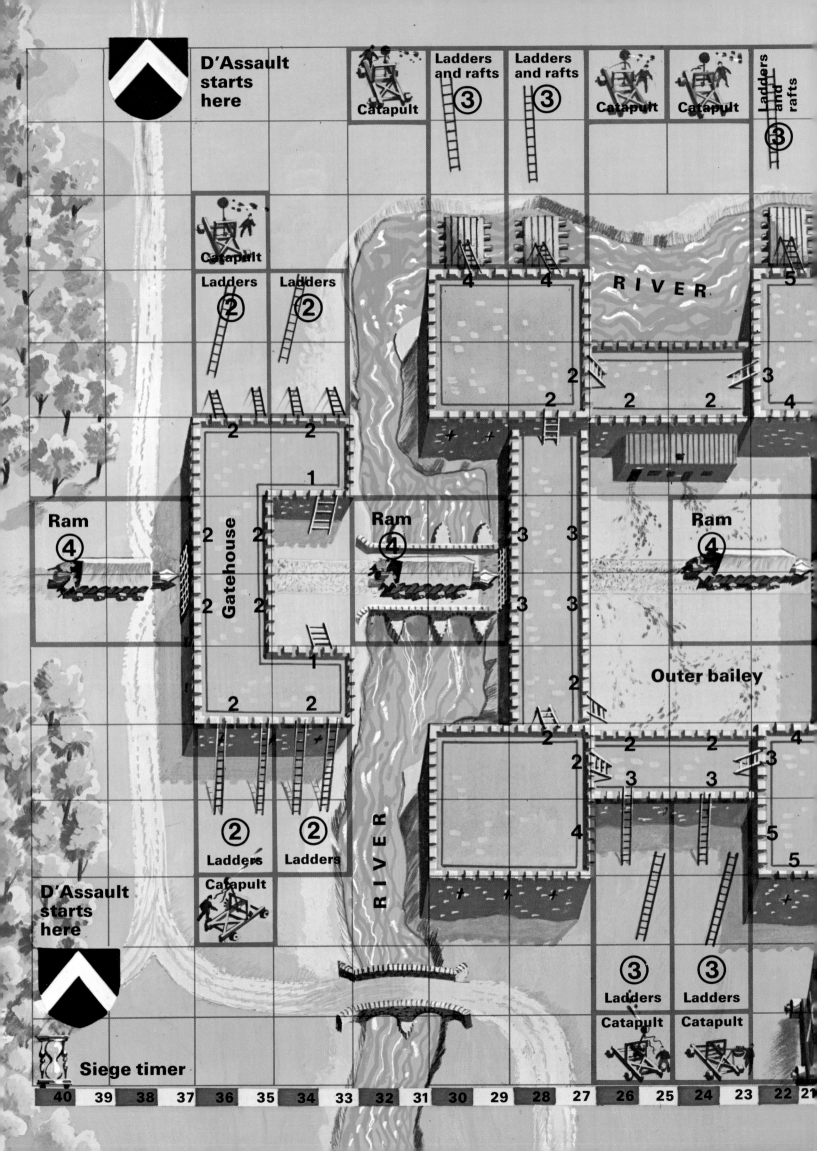

The board for **'Border Raiders'**
is on the other side. Remove it
with the rest of the pull-out
section by opening the staples in
the middle of the book.
You could use thin card to
strengthen this board and make
it last longer. Cut some card the
same size as the board and then
glue it to the plain side. You
could also cover it with
transparent, sticky-backed
plastic.

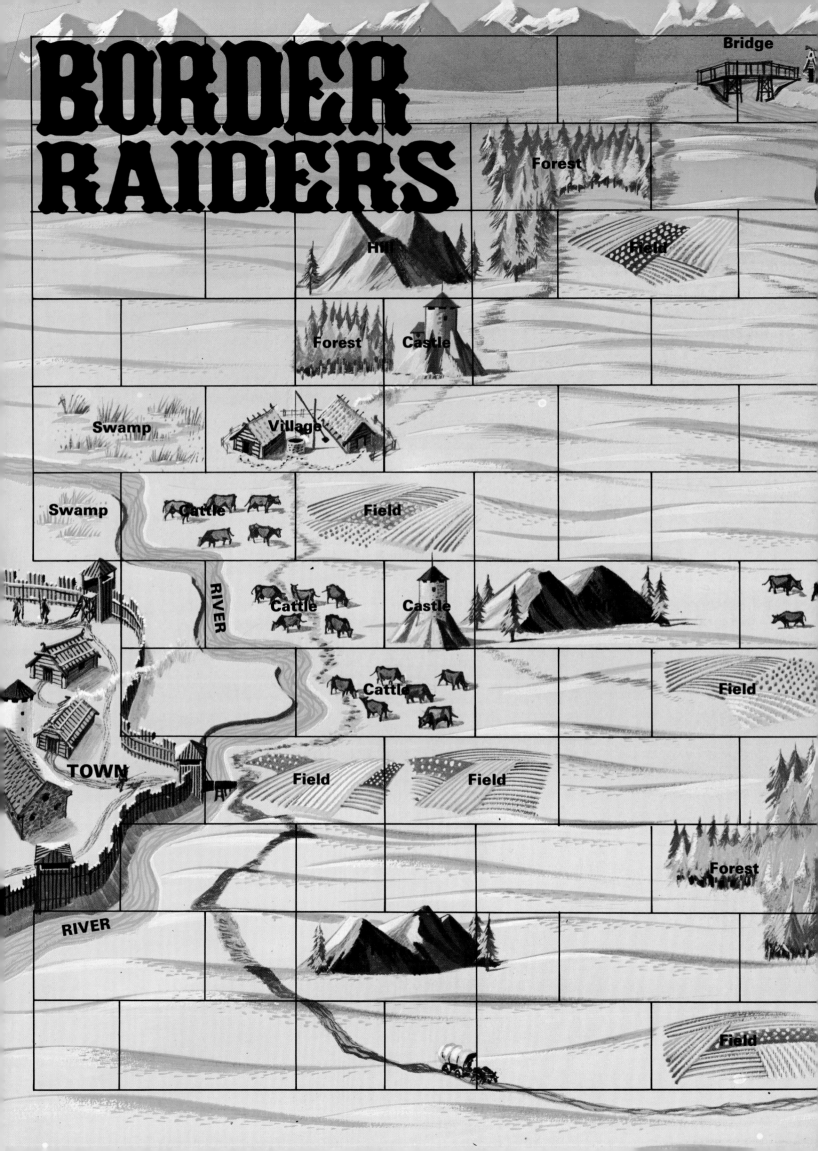

The board for **'Tournament'** is on the other side. Remove it with the rest of the pull-out section by opening the staples in the middle of the book. You could use thin card to strengthen this board and make it last longer. Cut some card the same size as the board and then glue it to the plain side. You could also cover it with transparent, sticky-backed plastic.

Tournament

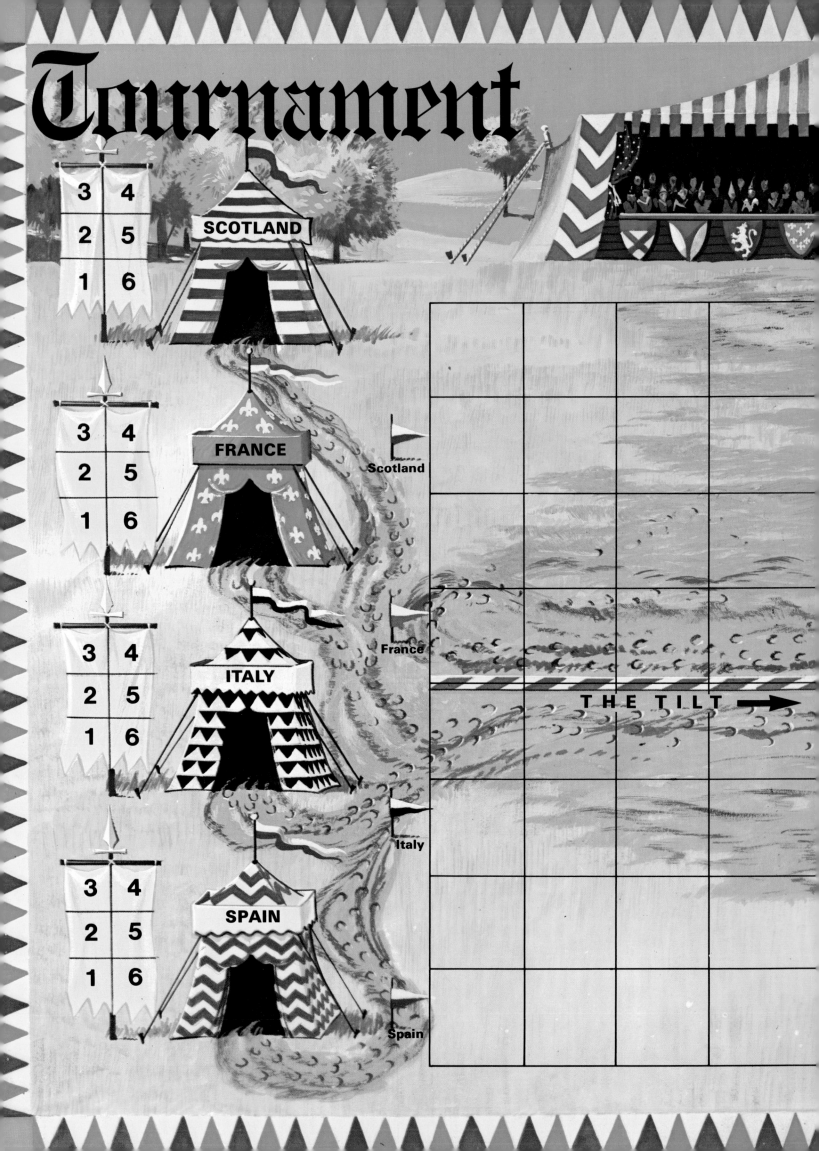

SCOTLAND

3   4
2   5
1   6

FRANCE

3   4
2   5
1   6

Scotland

ITALY

3   4
2   5
1   6

France

Italy

SPAIN

3   4
2   5
1   6

Spain

T H E   T I L T ➔

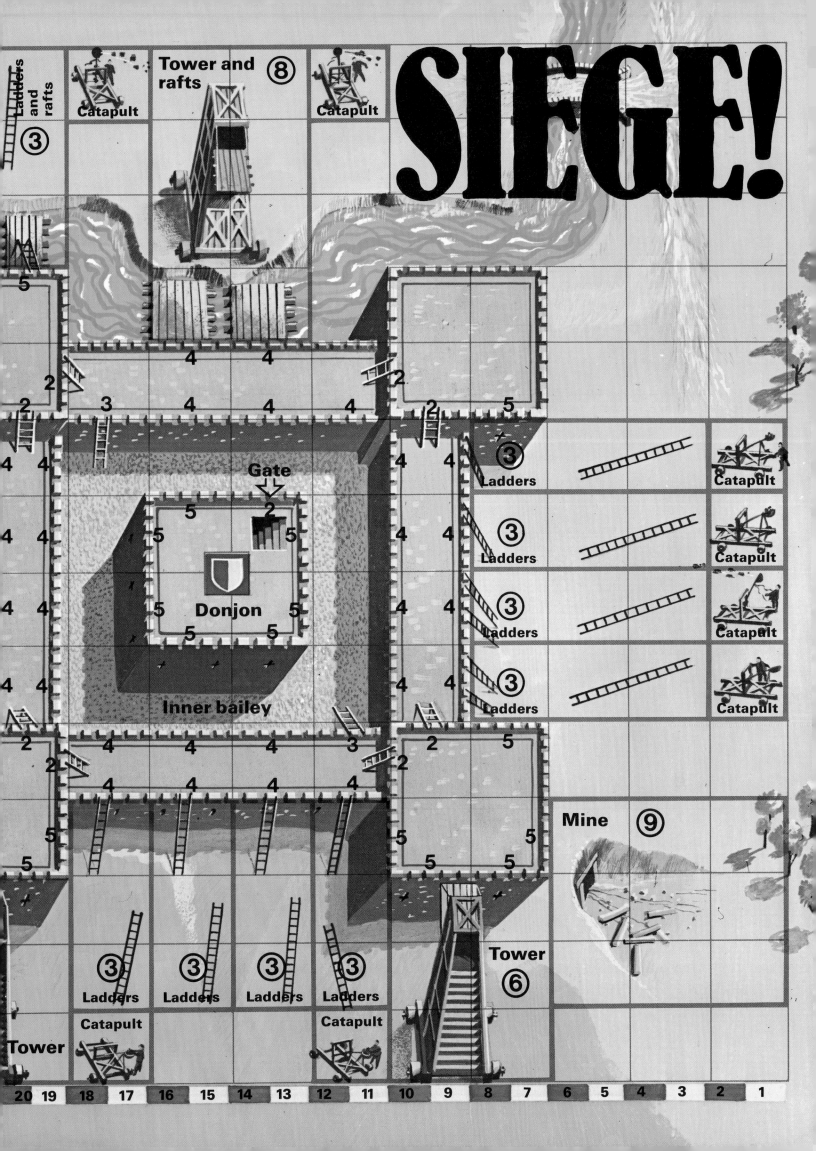

S E A

River

CROSSING
POINTS

ROAD

Crusader camp

MARSH OF
BIRKET-
RAMADAN

FOREST OF ARSOUF

Stream

**Rules
reminder**

All Moslêms move up to 3 spaces a turn

All knights move up to 2 spaces a turn

Infantry and baggage move up to 2 spaces
a turn on the road, but only 1 space a turn
elsewhere.

THE PIECES FOR BORDER RAIDERS

MEN-AT-ARMS

BLACK KARL KNIGHT

ARCHERS

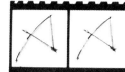

} RAIDER'S PIECES

MEN-AT-ARMS

DUKE CONRAD KNIGHT

ARCHERS

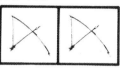

} DEFENDER'S PIECES

    SHEEP

    CATTLE

ATTACK MARKERS—USE THESE TO SHOW WHICH FIELDS AND VILLAGES HAVE BEEN ATTACKED.

THE PIECES FOR Tournament

SWEEP 5	SWEEP 5	SWEEP 5	SWEEP 5	
BODY 3	BODY 3	BODY 3	BODY 3	AIMING MARKERS
HELM 1	HELM 1	HELM 1	HELM 1	

FIT THE KNIGHTS TO THEIR HORSES LIKE THIS →

FIX WITH TAPE

BEND

HORSES

| BURGUNDY | ENGLAND | FRANCE | SCOTLAND | FLANDERS | GERMANY | SPAIN | ITALY |

KNIGHTS

Cut-out game pieces for **'Border Raiders'** and **'Tournament'** are on the other side of this page. Remove them with the rest of the pull-out section by opening the staples in the middle of the book.

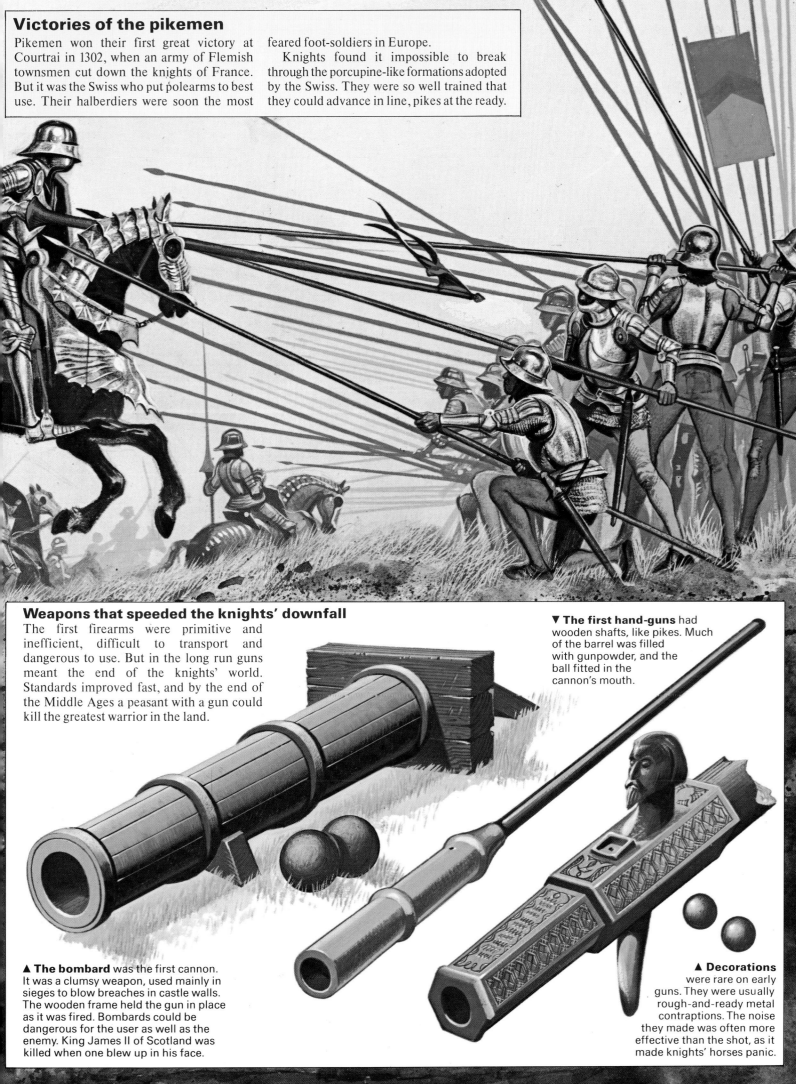

Victories of the pikemen

Pikemen won their first great victory at Courtrai in 1302, when an army of Flemish townsmen cut down the knights of France. But it was the Swiss who put polearms to best use. Their halberdiers were soon the most feared foot-soldiers in Europe.

Knights found it impossible to break through the porcupine-like formations adopted by the Swiss. They were so well trained that they could advance in line, pikes at the ready.

Weapons that speeded the knights' downfall

The first firearms were primitive and inefficient, difficult to transport and dangerous to use. But in the long run guns meant the end of the knights' world. Standards improved fast, and by the end of the Middle Ages a peasant with a gun could kill the greatest warrior in the land.

▼ **The first hand-guns** had wooden shafts, like pikes. Much of the barrel was filled with gunpowder, and the ball fitted in the cannon's mouth.

▲ **The bombard** was the first cannon. It was a clumsy weapon, used mainly in sieges to blow breaches in castle walls. The wooden frame held the gun in place as it was fired. Bombards could be dangerous for the user as well as the enemy. King James II of Scotland was killed when one blew up in his face.

▲ **Decorations** were rare on early guns. They were usually rough-and-ready metal contraptions. The noise they made was often more effective than the shot, as it made knights' horses panic.

TIMECHART: 1060-1492

This timechart shows many of the important events that shaped the history of the Middle Ages. Use it as a reference to pinpoint the things described in the rest of the book.

1060	Norman knights under Robert Guiscard begin the conquest of Sicily. They already control most of southern Italy.
1066	William, Duke of Normandy, wins Battle of Hastings and begins the conquest of England. English lands given to Norman and French knights.
1071	Seljuk Turks conquer Jerusalem. Byzantines defeated at Manzikert.
1084	Norman knights under Robert Guiscard capture and sack Rome, defended by Germans. Pope Gregory VII (Hildebrand) rescued from captivity.
1095	Council of Clermont – Pope Urban II calls for the First Crusade.
1096	Crusaders set out for the Holy Land.
1099	Jerusalem captured by the crusaders. Kingdom of Jerusalem founded. El Cid dies in battle against the Moslems in Spain.
1118	Military order of Templars founded.
1147	Second Crusade. German crusaders defeated by the Turks at Dorylaeum.
1171	Saladin becomes ruler in Egypt. Henry II of England conquers Ireland.
1189	Third Crusade led by Richard I of England and Philip II of France.
1190	Teutonic Knights founded. Frederick Barbarossa drowned on crusade.
1194	Henry VI of Germany conquers Sicily.
1204	Philip II of France conquers Normandy and Maine. Constantinople taken by western knights, led by French and Venetians, on the Fourth Crusade.
1212	Battle of Las Navas de Tolosa – Spanish knights utterly defeat Moslems.
1214	Battle of Bouvines – great victory of French knights over Germans and English.
1248	Sixth Crusade led by St Louis, King of France. He attacks the Moslems in Egypt.
1250	Crusaders defeated at Battle of Mansurah. King Louis captured.
1283	Teutonic Knights complete the conquest of Prussia.
1302	Battle of Courtrai – French knights defeated by Flemish infantry.
1313	Invention of gunpowder in Germany.
1314	Battle of Bannockburn – English knights defeated by King Robert of Scotland.
1337	Hundred Years War begins between France and England.
1346	Battle of Crécy – English longbowmen defeat French knights.
1382	Battle of Roosebeke – French knights win massive victory over Flemings.
1386	Battle of Sempach – Swiss infantry defeat Austrian knights.
1410	Battle of Tannenberg – Teutonic knights defeated by the Poles.
1415	Battle of Agincourt – English longbowmen defeat French knights.
1420	Battle near Prague – Hussites under Zizka defeat German and Hungarian knights.
1429	Joan of Arc relieves siege of Orléans.
1453	Hundred Years War ends at the Battle of Castillon – English defeated. Constantinople captured by the Turks.
1455	Wars of the Roses start in England. Battle of St Albans.
1457	Marienburg, centre of the Teutonic Knights, captured by the Poles.
1476	Battles of Grandson and Morat – last great victories of the Swiss infantry.
1485	Battle of Bosworth – end of Wars of Roses in England.
1492	Fall of Granada – the last Moslem stronghold in Spain. Columbus discovers America.

IMPROVING AND STORING GAME PIECES

The pieces for each battlegame are designed to be cut out and used as they are. They will last a long time if you strengthen them with thin card as shown in the illustration below.

The best card to use is the sort that postcards are printed on. Glue the pieces onto the card, either separately or in groups, and carefully cut them out with a craft knife or scissors.

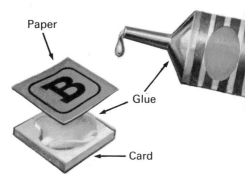

You will need to store the pieces in a safe place, otherwise some will get lost. Use an envelope or a small cardboard box for each game's pieces. Mark the name of the game on the front. Keep all four sets in a drawer or on a shelf.

Making your own pieces

When you are used to playing the games, you may wish to use more exciting and colourful pieces than the paper pieces supplied with this book.

With some practice you can make your own pieces out of card. You can cut them to the shape of the various people and animals used in the games. Enamel modelling paints are best for colouring, as they give a hard-wearing glossy finish.

A good idea is to use miniature figures on the gameboards. They can be bought from any good model shop. They are made in a lot of different sizes, so you can choose the right ones to fit the different gameboards.

Knights on chargers will make 'Tournament' livelier. Use models of knights on foot for the hand-to-hand combats.

Knights on horseback are also good for 'The Battle of Arsouf' and 'Border Raiders'. Paint each side's men a different colour, and mark the fighting value on each piece. You can buy animal models of sheep and cattle for 'Border Raiders', and of mules and oxen for the baggage pieces of 'The Battle of Arsouf'.

A crusader game for two players.

As dawn breaks on September 7, 1191, Saladin's Moslem army lies in wait to attack the crusader force of Richard Lionheart. The crusaders know they must fight their way through to the friendly town of Arsouf. Will they succeed, or will Saladin's lighter-armed but faster-moving men prevent them?

1 The pieces

PIECES		FIGHTING VALUE *F.V.*	MOVES *EACH TURN*
THE CRUSADER ARMY	1 SQUADRON OF KNIGHTS TEMPLARS	4	} UP TO 2 SPACES
	1 " " " HOSPITALLERS	4	
	3 SQUADRONS OF KNIGHTS	3	
	6 TROOPS OF INFANTRY	2	} UP TO 2 SPACES ON THE ROAD. I SPACE ELSEWHERE ON THE BOARD.
	4 BAGGAGE TRAINS	1	
	RICHARD LIONHEART	2 AND ADDS 2 TO ANY PIECE HE IS ADJACENT TO	UP TO 2 SPACES
THE MOSLEM ARMY	4 SQUADRONS OF MAMELUKES	3	} UP TO 3 SPACES
	6 TROOPS OF HORSE-ARCHERS	2	
	5 " " SKIRMISHERS	1	
	SALADIN	2 AND ADDS 2 TO ANY PIECE HE IS ADJACENT TO	}

2 Extras
A dice (or use the spinner provided)

3 Object of the game
One player controls the crusader army of Richard Lionheart, the other controls the Moslem army of Saladin.

The crusaders must get 2 baggage pieces and any 2 other pieces to Arsouf.

The Moslems must stop them.

4 How to start
Choose sides. The player controlling the crusader army places all his pieces in the camp marked at the top-right corner of the board.

The player controlling the Moslem army places all his pieces in the area marked at the bottom-left corner of the board.

The river in front of the crusader camp can only be crossed at the ford. Pieces can wade over the stream at any point.

No piece can enter the Marsh of Birket-Ramadan.

The crusader player takes the first turn.

5 Moving
Both players can move as many pieces as they wish each turn. Only one piece can be in a space at a time.

The maximum number of spaces each piece can move per turn is given in section 1.

6 Attacking
After a player has moved all the pieces he wishes to move, he can announce attacks. A piece can attack any enemy piece on an adjoining space. Players can attack with as many pieces as are in a position to do so, but each piece can only make **one** attack a turn.

The attacking player throws the dice, and adds the fighting value of his piece to the number thrown.

The defending player then throws the dice. He adds the fighting value of his piece to the number thrown, and also adds **half** the fighting value of any other of his pieces on spaces adjoining the attacking piece.

> Either player can add 2 to the fighting value of his piece if the leader (Richard Lionheart for the crusaders, Saladin for the Moslems) is on an adjoining space.

The piece with the higher total wins. The losing piece is 'wounded' and is laid on its side. If the two totals are the same, both pieces remain as they are.

A wounded piece cannot attack, but can defend itself if attacked – its fighting value remains the same.

If attacked and defeated a second time, it is 'killed'. The piece is removed from the board.

Wounded pieces can move 1 space per turn. They 'recover' if there are no enemy pieces within 3 spaces. They are placed upright again, and can move and attack normally.

HOW TO ADD UP ATTACK AND DEFENCE SCORES

EXAMPLE

ATTACKER THROWS DICE AND ADDS HIS OWN *F.V.* TO THE SCORE

DEFENDER THROWS DICE AND ADDS HIS *F.V.* PLUS HALF THE *F.V.* OF HIS MEN NEXT TO THE ATTACKER (X,X) BUT *NOT* IF THEY ARE WOUNDED.

7 Charging
Crusader knights who attack Moslem pieces after 'charging' 2 spaces directly at them add 1 to their fighting value.

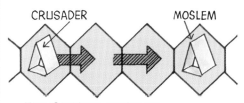

CRUSADER   MOSLEM

THE CHARGE MUST BE IN A STRAIGHT LINE.

8 Tips on tactics
● The crusaders must protect their weak baggage pieces. In the real battle, Richard kept the baggage train near the sea, protected by a shield of infantry and knights.
● In real life, Saladin did his best to encircle the crusaders, attacking all along the line and in the rear. Try doing the same.
● Put Saladin and Richard next to their strongest men.

A game for two players.

Warrior earl Eustace d'Assault has long cast envious eyes on the lands of his neighbour, Baron Hugh de Fender. When de Fender falls ill, d'Assault decides to act. He calls out his knights on the 40 days' military service owed him as his feudal due. Can d'Assault take de Fender's castle in the 40 days, or will the baron hold out until d'Assault's army breaks up?

1 The pieces

| Eustace d'Assault |
| 19 attacking knights |
| Hugh de Fender |
| 10 defending knights |
| 6 weapon pieces |
| (Greek fire, boiling oil, rocks) |

2 Extras
A dice
A counter
Used matchsticks

3 Object of the game
One player controls Eustace d'Assault and his army; the other player controls the army of Hugh de Fender.

To win, d'Assault's men must fight their way into the donjon of the castle and seize de Fender before the 40 days run out.

If they have not succeeded by then, de Fender wins.

4 Setting up the pieces
Choose sides. The player controlling the army of de Fender places his men anywhere within the castle. The piece representing de Fender must be placed in the donjon, where it remains throughout the game.

The weapon pieces are kept at the side of the board, ready for placing in the course of the game.

D'Assault's men start the game off the board.

Set the counter at '40' on the siege timer.

5 Starting the game
D'Assault moves first. His men must enter the board – one through each of the two entrance squares per turn.

All men move one square a turn. Diagonal moves are not allowed. Each player can move all, some or none of his men each turn. Only one man can be on a square at a time (except for weapon pieces – see 7).

Move the counter on the siege timer down a day every time de Fender finishes a turn.

6 Getting into the castle
D'Assault's men must use siege engines (battering-rams, scaling ladders etc.) to get into the castle. These are marked on the board. They only come into operation when manned by the specified number of knights – to use a siege tower, for instance, d'Assault must position six pieces in the six squares outlined.

Once a siege engine is fully-manned, it can be used to launch an attack. It can be used for attacking for the rest of the game, even when only one or two men are on it.

Place a used matchstick by the engine to show that it has been fully-manned.

Attacks are made at the start of a turn.

To make an attack, d'Assault indicates the square he is attacking and throws the dice. He adds the number thrown to the point value of the siege engine (which is the same as the number of men needed to man it – e.g. 6 for a siege tower.) He can add 1 extra point if one of his men is manning a catapult adjoining the siege engine. He can add 2 extra points for any other of his men in contact with a knight defending the square.

The defender does **not** throw the dice. He counts the defensive value of the wall square attacked (as marked on the wall), adding 3 for a weapon piece if one has been placed on the square under attack (see 7).

For the attack to succeed, the attacking player must score **3 points more** than the defender. If he succeeds, the defending knight on the square under attack must retreat one square in any direction. Knights cannot retreat from the wall to the bailey unless a ladder is marked on the board. If the knight cannot retreat he is 'killed' and removed from the board. If the attack fails, both knights remain in place.

For example: D'Assault's men are manning a siege tower and an adjoining catapult. D'Assault throws a 3. His total is 6 + 1 + 3 = 10.

De Fender has placed a boiling oil piece on the square attacked, which has a defensive value of 4. His total is 4 + 3 = 7.

D'Assault has 3 more points so his attack succeeds.

NOTE: If a battering-ram attack succeeds, d'Assault's men pass directly under the wall squares to the first squares in the courtyard. Two men per turn through the gate.

7 Weapon pieces
De Fender can place his weapon pieces anywhere on the castle walls at the **end** of any of his turns. Weapon pieces cannot be placed in the donjon.

Once a piece has been placed, it cannot be moved. Any man of either side can move into squares occupied by weapon pieces.

Weapon pieces have a value of 3. They only count when manned by a knight on the same square as them. They can be used by any knight to attack an enemy knight on a lower level or on a siege engine.

MANNING WEAPONS
A WEAPON PIECE IS MANNED BY PLACING A KNIGHT ON TOP OF IT.

---

8 Hand-to-hand fighting
Once d'Assault's men get inside the castle, any knight on either side can attack an enemy knight on an adjoining square, provided that they are on the same level or connected by a ladder. Attacks take place at the **start** of a turn.

The attacking player throws the dice. He must get 3 or more to win. If he gets 3 or more, the losing knight must retreat one square in any direction. If he cannot retreat he is killed. If the attacker gets less than 3, both pieces remain in place.

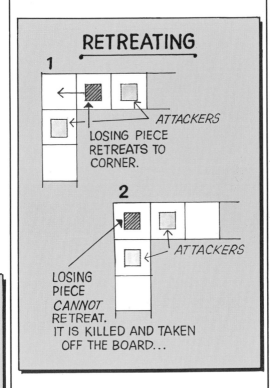

RETREATING

1 ATTACKERS. LOSING PIECE RETREATS TO CORNER.

2 ATTACKERS. LOSING PIECE CANNOT RETREAT. IT IS KILLED AND TAKEN OFF THE BOARD...

9 Tips on tactics
● De Fender should wait to see where d'Assault plans to attack before placing weapon pieces. He cannot afford to waste them.
● Fight for control of the walls around the inner bailey. It is hard for d'Assault's men to enter the donjon if de Fender's men are on the walls.
● Try to trap enemy knights where they cannot retreat before attacking them.

EARL D'ASSAULT JOINS IN THE ATTACK WITH HIS MEN, BUT DE FENDER STAYS IN THE DONJON

A game for two players.

The scene is the eastern border country of Germany in the 13th Century. Karl the Black, renegade Count of Grimmigen, is launching a raid on the lands of his neighbour, Duke Conrad. As Conrad's men gather, Karl's marauders burn fields, raid villages and take sheep and cattle. Will the Duke's troops be able to repel them and save their lands from pillage?

1 The pieces

PIECES	FIGHTING VALUE(F.V.)	MOVES *EACH TURN*
KARL THE BLACK		
1 GROUP OF KNIGHTS	6	UP TO 2 SPACES
6 LEVIES OF MEN-AT-ARMS	6	" "
2 BANDS OF ARCHERS	3	UP TO 3 SPACES
	2	" 4 SPACES
DUKE CONRAD		
1 GROUP OF KNIGHTS	6	UP TO 2 SPACES
6 LEVIES OF MEN-AT-ARMS	6	" "
2 BANDS OF ARCHERS	3	UP TO 3 SPACES
	2	" 4 SPACES
4 HERDS OF CATTLE	—	} UP TO 2 SPACES
4 FLOCKS OF SHEEP	—	} *(WHEN HERDED.)*
ATTACK MARKERS	—	—

2 Extras
A dice

3 Object of the game
Karl wins the game if his men attack half of Conrad's property – at least 5 fields and 3 villages – and take half the livestock to Castle Grimmigen – at least 2 flocks of sheep and 2 herds of cattle.

Conrad wins the game by preventing Karl's men from doing this.

4 Starting the game
Players choose sides.

The player controlling Karl the Black's men places them all in Castle Grimmigen. The player controlling Duke Conrad's men places five of his men in the town. He puts the rest in castles, one to a castle.

5 Playing the game
The two players take turns to move. Karl starts. Players can move all, some or none of their pieces each turn.

Each player may have up to **four** of his pieces in the same space at a time.

6 Moving
The number of spaces each piece can move is listed in section 1.

No piece can move through or into hill spaces. Rivers must be crossed by bridges or fords. Only archers can move through forests and swamps.

Karl's men cannot move through or into castles or the town. Conrad's men cannot cross the border into Grimmigen. Karl's men cannot attack Conrad's castles or pieces inside them.

THIS COUNTS AS A 3 SPACE MOVE

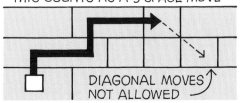

DIAGONAL MOVES NOT ALLOWED

7 Plundering
Karl's men attack fields and villages by moving into the spaces representing them and staying for the rest of that turn.

Sheep and cattle must be herded back to Castle Grimmigen.

To burn a field: 2 of Karl's men must move into it.

To attack a village: 4 of Karl's men must move into it.

To take sheep and cattle: 2 of Karl's men must 'herd' the animals back to Castle Grimmigen. When herding, pieces move up to 2 spaces a turn.

Fields and villages can only be attacked once. Place a marker piece on each field or village destroyed as a reminder that it cannot be attacked again.

HERDING ANIMALS

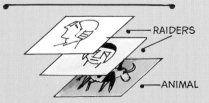

RAIDERS

ANIMAL

TWO OF THE RAIDERS MOVE WITH THE ANIMAL PIECE AT TWO SPACES PER TURN UNTIL THEY REACH CASTLE GRIMMIGEN, IF ONE OR BOTH OF THE HERDERS LEAVE THE ANIMAL BEFORE REACHING THE CASTLE, THE ANIMAL MOVES BACK TO ITS OWN SPACE AT TWO SPACES PER TURN.

8 Fighting
Players attack by moving pieces into a space occupied by enemy men.

Each player throws the dice once for each of his men in the space, and adds up the total of the dice throws. He then adds the total fighting value of the pieces. He divides the sum total by 4. His men 'kill' enemy pieces on the space with fighting values up to the final figure. 'Killed' pieces are removed from the board.

The loser retreats. Conrad's men retreat to the nearest castle. Karl's men retreat 2 spaces in any direction as long as the move does not put them in position to attack in their following turn.

9 Archers
Archers can fire at enemy pieces from one space away. The attacking player throws the dice **once** for each archer firing. If he throws a 6, one enemy piece is killed – the attacking player chooses which one if there are several in the space. If he throws any other number, the arrow has missed and play continues.

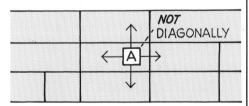

NOT DIAGONALLY

AN ARCHER CAN FIRE AT ENEMY TROOPS IN THESE SPACES.

10 Tips on tactics
● Place archers in forests and swamps where they can fire at passing pieces but can only be attacked by other archers.
● Never let your men be surprised by a stronger force, or they will risk being massacred.

ATTACKING~
HOW TO CALCULATE ENEMY LOSSES

EXAMPLE

ATTACKER HAS	DICE THROW	F.V.
1 KNIGHT	2	6
2 MEN-AT-ARMS	1, 3	3, 3
1 ARCHER	4	2
TOTALS	10 +	14 = (24)
FINAL SCORE	24÷4 =	**6**

ATTACKER CAN TAKE AWAY ENEMY PIECES WITH AN F.V. UP TO A TOTAL VALUE OF 6 · EG · 1 KNIGHT, OR 2 MEN-AT-ARMS.

A jousting game for two or four players.

It is late in the fourteenth century. The Duke of Burgundy has invited the finest knights in Europe to a grand tournament in his lands in Flanders. It is to last for three days. By the end of the final day, one of the knights will have vanquished all rivals to become supreme champion.

1 The pieces
8 knights
8 horses, one for each knight
4 sets of 3 target markers – 1 sweep (value 5), 1 body (value 3), 1 helm (value 1)

2 Extras
A dice (or use the spinner provided)
8 counters (to be used as prowess markers)

3 Object of the game
The player whose knight or knights emerge victorious from the melée on the final day of the tournament wins the game.

If more than one of his knights remain, they can fight a courtesy joust to settle which is the supreme champion.

4 How to start
Choose a team of knights. If two people are playing, each has four knights. If four people are playing, each has two knights.

Place the knights on their horses in front of their tents.

Each player takes one set of target markers, and a counter for each knight. The counter is used to mark the knight's prowess rating (how good he is) on the pennant next to his tent. Each knight starts with a rating of 1.

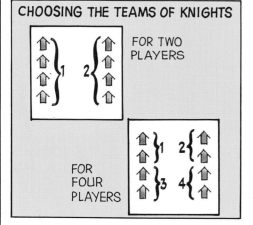

CHOOSING THE TEAMS OF KNIGHTS

FOR TWO PLAYERS

FOR FOUR PLAYERS

5 The first day – the challenge joust
Each players throws the dice. The one with the highest score chooses one of his knights to make the first challenge.

The knight challenges one of the knights on the opposite side of the board. The two knights fight a joust (see 6).

The losing player then challenges the winning knight with another knight.

When all of a player's knights have been defeated, the challenge moves to the next undefeated knight clockwise round the board. The day ends when every knight has jousted.

Place all knights back on their horses ready for the second day's jousting.

6 Jousting
1 Each player chooses a target marker (helm, body or sweep) for his knight, keeping it face down.

2 The two knights take up position at opposite ends of the tilt.

3 Each player throws the dice. The one with the higher score moves his knight the number of pips shown on the dice along the tilt. The other knight is then moved onto the square diagonally opposite. If the dice throw is equal, throw again.

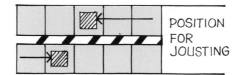

POSITION FOR JOUSTING

4 Each player now reveals the target marker he has chosen. Helm hits before body, and body before sweep. The knight who hits first counts up his total, adding his target marker score, his prowess rating and the number of squares he has moved. If the total is 10 or more, his opponent is unhorsed and retires to his tent.

If the total is less than 10, he has missed. His opponent then adds up his own score. If his total is 10 or more, the other knight is unhorsed.

5 If both players have chosen the same target marker, both add up their knights' totals. The knight with the higher total unhorses his rival – if the total is 10 or more. If neither scores 10 or more, the two knights have missed one another, and they joust again.

6 The prowess rating of the winning knight is increased by 1.

7 The second day – the knock-out joust
The second day's jousting is an elimination contest. Each time a knight wins a joust, his prowess rating continues to go up 1, up to a maximum of 6.

Jousting order: Each knight starts by jousting against the knight opposite (Flanders vs. Scotland, etc.). The winner of joust 1 then fights the winner of joust 3, and the winner of joust 2 fights the winner of joust 4. The two remaining knights then fight the final.

Place the knights back on their horses ready for the melée.

8 The third day – the melée
1 The melée begins with a joust. Put each knight on the square next to the small pennant at the side of the field. Each knight jousts against the knight opposite, across the lists and **not** along the tilt. All knights remain in the lists after the joust. Winning knights continue charging to the square at the edge of the board. Losers are unhorsed and remain in the square where they fell.

2 When the round of jousting has been completed, the melée proper begins.

From this point on, target markers are no longer used, and prowess ratings remain as they are.

Moving: Knights on horseback can either manoeuvre for two squares (see diagram) or they can charge. Charging knights can move any number of squares in a straight line.

Knights on foot can move up to 2 squares in any direction.

No knight can move through or onto an occupied square. Diagonal moves are not allowed.

KNIGHTS CAN MANOEUVRE FOR TWO SQUARES OR CHARGE THE LENGTH OF THE LISTS.

POSSIBLE ATTACK POSITIONS

Attacking: Knights attack from adjoining squares (see diagram) after moving.

If a mounted knight attacks a mounted knight: The two knights charge one another, moving 1 square each alternately until they meet midway. The attacker throws the dice, and adds the number thrown to his prowess rating and the number of squares he has charged. If he scores 10 or more, his opponent is unhorsed. If he gets less, he has missed and both knights continue charging until their path is blocked by another knight or the edge of the lists.

If a mounted knight attacks a knight on foot: The attacker throws the dice, and adds the number thrown to his knight's prowess rating and the number of squares he has charged. If he scores 10 or more, his opponent is removed from play. If he scores less, he has missed and the knight on foot remains in place. In either case the mounted knight continues charging until his path is blocked.

If a knight on foot attacks a mounted knight: The attacker throws the dice and adds his knight's prowess rating to the number thrown. If he scores 10 or more, the rider is unhorsed. Both knights remain in place.

If a knight on foot attacks a knight on foot: Each player throws the dice, and adds his knight's prowess rating to the number thrown. The knight with the higher score remains in place, and the loser is removed from play.

In any attack: add 3 points to the attacker's score if he has one or more team-mates also in squares adjoining the defending knight.

9 Tips on tactics
● When jousting, choose the sweep for knights with low prowess ratings.
● In the melée, remember to use your knights as a team. Knights on foot can be used to gang up on opponents and to box in knights on horseback.

RICHARD AND SALADIN

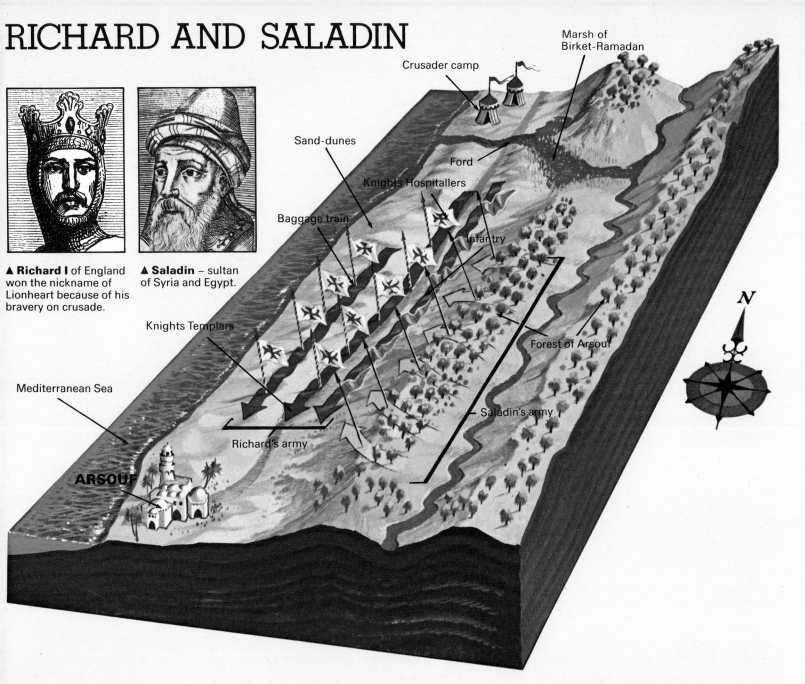

Crusader camp

Marsh of Birket-Ramadan

Sand-dunes

Ford

Knights Hospitallers

Baggage train

Infantry

Knights Templars

Forest of Arsouf

Saladin's army

Mediterranean Sea

Richard's army

ARSOUF

N

▲ **Richard I** of England won the nickname of Lionheart because of his bravery on crusade.

▲ **Saladin** – sultan of Syria and Egypt.

▲ The Battle of Arsouf

1 After resting for a day in camp, protected by the Marsh of Birket-Ramadan, Richard and his army set out on the seventeenth day of their march from Acre to a new base at Jaffa.

2 Hidden in the Forest of Arsouf, the Moslem army of Saladin waited for the crusaders to come into sight.

3 On the six-mile march to Arsouf, Richard's baggage train marched next to the sea. The knights rode down the road. The infantry, crossbows at the ready, protected the column's flank.

4 Saladin's army attacked, as Richard had known it would. The crusader column held firm, and kept moving towards Arsouf. Richard was waiting for the right moment to counter-attack.

5 For an hour or more the Knights Hospitallers in the rear endured the arrows and lances of the enemy without breaking ranks. Then, losing patience, they charged. Richard ordered the rest of his knights to follow them. Caught in a confused mass, the Moslems stood little chance. After three charges they were routed.

Richard I of England – the Lionheart – and his enemy Saladin were both brilliant military leaders.

Saladin managed to unite the many different Moslem states. In 1187, four years before Richard arrived in the Holy Land, he had recaptured Jerusalem from the Crusaders. He was a bold and shrewd commander, and was admired even by his enemies for chivalry.

When Jerusalem fell to Saladin, the rulers of the west had patched up their differences and joined to launch the Third Crusade. Richard and Philip Augustus of France set sail for Palestine. The German emperor, Frederick Barbarossa, took an army of 100,000 men by land. But he was drowned while crossing a river in Turkey, and his army broke up.

Victory at Acre

The first aim of the crusaders was to help the Christian army besieging Acre. The arrival of fresh forces compelled Saladin, who was trying to relieve the city, to withdraw. The town soon fell to the crusaders, who slaughtered its inhabitants.

Shortly after the capture of Acre, Philip sailed back to France, leaving Richard as sole commander of the crusader armies. His next goal was Jerusalem, and he set out southwards from Acre along the coast.

Saladin attacks

When Saladin tried to attack Richard at Arsouf, he was heavily defeated. The crusaders reached Jaffa, the nearest seaport to Jerusalem, safely.

The defeat at Arsouf made Saladin realize that he could not defeat the Christian knights in open battle. Richard in turn realized that as long as his men quarrelled among themselves they could never defeat the Moslems inland, near Jerusalem.

So Richard did the sensible thing. He made an agreement with Saladin. The Christians kept the coastal towns, and were allowed to visit Jerusalem as pilgrims

This truce did not last for long. Both Richard and Saladin died within a few years. War started again, and there were several more crusades before the Christians were finally driven out of Palestine in 1291.

SIEGE WAR

Sieges of castles and towns were an important part of wars in the Middle Ages. To stand up to a siege the people inside the castle had to have plenty of food and water. The walls of their castle had to be in good repair.

The attacker could not always surround the castle and wait for the defenders to run out of food. There might be an army on its way to rescue the defenders. His men might have less food than the people inside. So it was always worth trying to take the castle quickly by force.

A lot of men would be killed in an attack on a strong castle. So attackers often promised to treat defenders well if they surrendered. If they refused they could expect no mercy when the castle fell.

The mechanics of siege warfare

1. **Belfry.** Besiegers built these movable towers with any wood they could find, including timber torn from nearby houses. A cover of animal hides gave some protection against arrows.

2. **Pitch, oil or water** was heated by the defenders and poured down on the attackers. Boiling liquids were particularly effective against men in armour.

3. **Mangonel.** This catapult-like engine was used by both defenders and attackers. Tightly twisted rope provided the force to hurl rocks and blazing missiles.

4. **Arrow slits.** Horizontal slits were for crossbows. The vertical slits were used by longbowmen.

5. **Wooden ladders** were often used to scale the walls. They were quick to put up, but could easily be pushed away or destroyed by defenders.

6. **Wall fortifications.** Stones could be dropped on attackers from machicolations. The sloping tops of crenellated walls reduced the chance of missiles fired by attackers bouncing onto defenders.

7. **Mine.** Walls were undermined by digging tunnels supported by wooden props. When the props were set on fire, the tunnel caved in, causing a section of the wall above to collapse.

8. **Mantlet.** This protective screen enabled bowmen to fire from close range at defenders on the castle walls.

9. **Battering-ram.** This was used against wooden gates or weak parts of the wall. It was usually a tree trunk with an iron head attached. The men who swung the ram were protected by a roof of timber or hide from boiling oil, stones and arrows.

10. **Thick mats** of woven reed or sticks were lowered on ropes by the defenders to lessen the impact of the battering-ram.

11. **Greek fire** was a flaming substance that could be hurled from catapults or squirted in a jet from bellows.

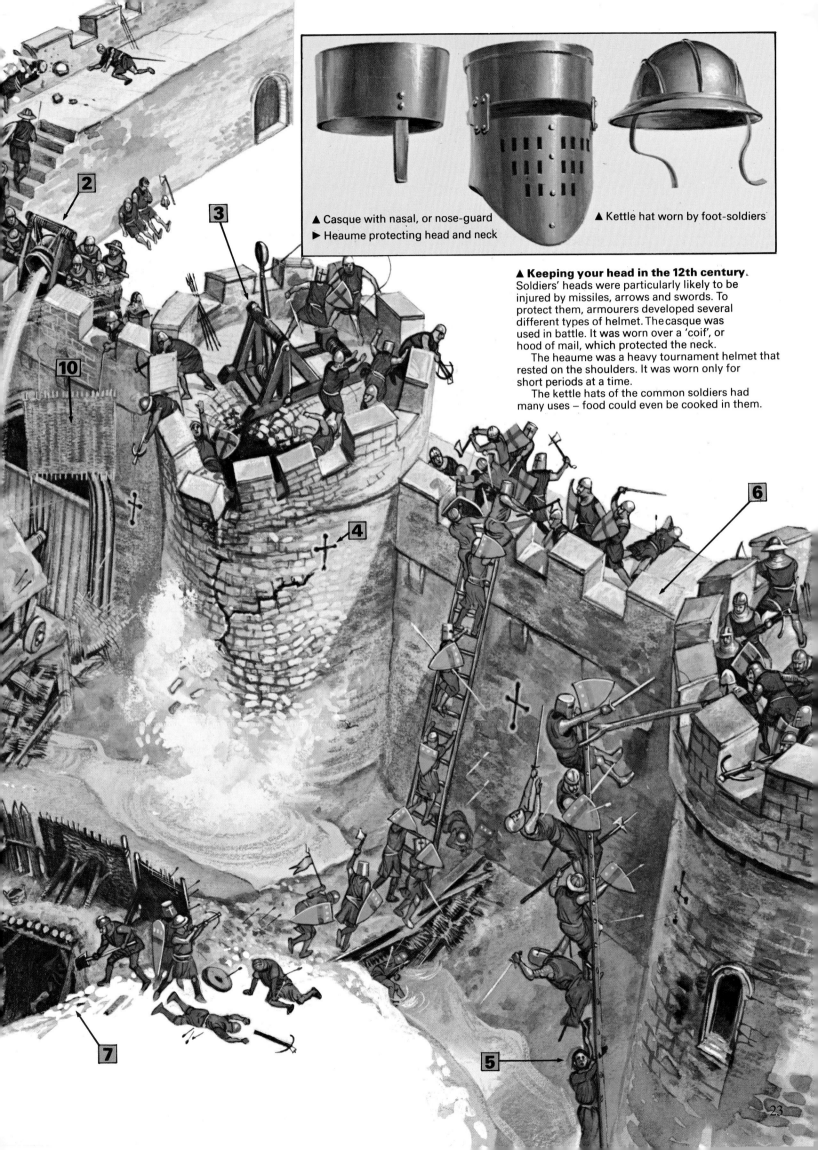

▲ Casque with nasal, or nose-guard
► Heaume protecting head and neck

▲ Kettle hat worn by foot-soldiers

▲ **Keeping your head in the 12th century.**
Soldiers' heads were particularly likely to be
injured by missiles, arrows and swords. To
protect them, armourers developed several
different types of helmet. The casque was
used in battle. It was worn over a 'coif', or
hood of mail, which protected the neck.

The heaume was a heavy tournament helmet that
rested on the shoulders. It was worn only for
short periods at a time.

The kettle hats of the common soldiers had
many uses – food could even be cooked in them.

WEAPONS OF THE MIDDLE AGES

The lance was the chief weapon used by knights in the charge. At first it was short and light enough to be thrown if necessary. Later it became larger and heavier. The longest lances were about 4.5m (15ft), but most were 3.5m (12ft) long.

The head of the lance was of metal and was triangular or lozenge-shaped. The shaft was made of a tough wood like ash or apple, and fitted into the head. Below the head was either a small crossbar or a pennant, to stop the lance going too far into the enemy's body. If it did, it would be difficult to pull out and the knight might fall off his horse.

The lance had to be held very tightly. It was not until the 1400s that a guard was fitted to protect the hand and give a better grip. This was called a vamplate. The lance was carried in the right hand and used across the horse's body, for better balance.

Fighting at close quarters
After the charge the knight fought at close quarters, chiefly with his sword. Every knight carried a sword. It was very important to him. Often there were holy relics inside the hilt.

It is not easy to make a sword that is good for both cutting and thrusting. Most knights chose cutting swords. These were flat and very heavy. But they could do little damage to a knight who was properly armed and trained to defend himself. This did not matter much. Taken alive, a knight could bring in a good ransom.

Crushing the enemy
But it was important to be able to kill foot-soldiers. With their arrows they were more of a danger. So knights needed weapons that were better than swords for killing. These can be called smashing or crushing weapons.

The axe was a favourite weapon with the Norsemen and the knights went on using it. A short-handled axe was best for fighting on horseback. King Robert of Scotland won a famous single combat against an English knight at Bannockburn using his battle-axe. A knight was in danger from an enemy with an axe unless he could unseat him first with his lance.

Another smashing weapon was the mace. This was a metal club with spikes on it or sharp edges. It could break the bones of a man in mail-armour.

Some knights also used the flail. This was a metal ball chained to a pole. It was useful for knocking down a shield. All these smashing weapons could only be used by strong men, after a lot of practice and at close quarters.

Weapons the knights feared
A knight had most to fear from the weapons of the foot-soldiers. An arrow from an English longbow could pierce even plate-armour. Historians have estimated that at the Battle of Crécy, in 1346, 30,000 arrows may have fallen on the French knights within the first minute.

The crossbow was at one time banned by the Church. Knights feared the terrible wounds it could cause them. But few people took any notice of the ban. The crossbow was slow to load and not as good as the English longbow. But it was a powerful weapon and could shoot very accurately. A man did not have to be very strong to use it.

Pikes and muskets
The weapons that finally drove the knight from the battlefield were the pike and the musket. These weapons could be used by foot-soldiers. Knights on horseback could not break through the long wall of pikes. The musketeers fired at them from behind the pikes.

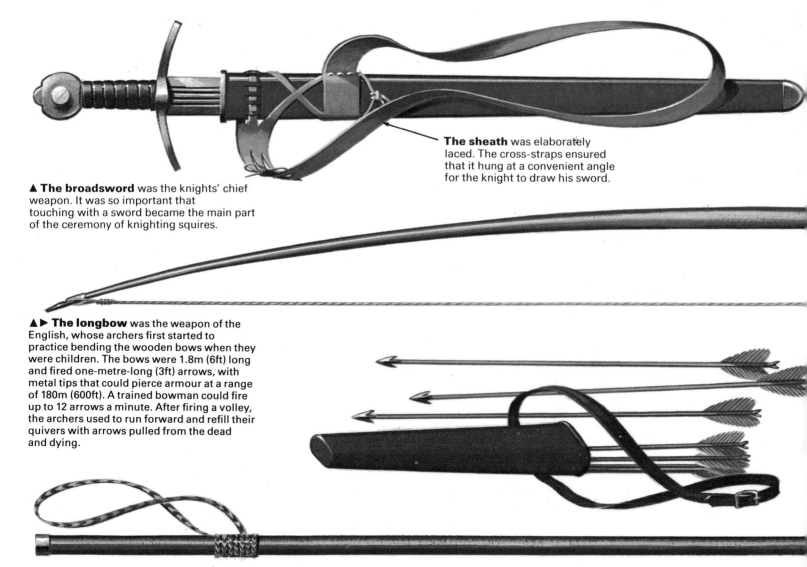

The sheath was elaborately laced. The cross-straps ensured that it hung at a convenient angle for the knight to draw his sword.

▲ **The broadsword** was the knights' chief weapon. It was so important that touching with a sword became the main part of the ceremony of knighting squires.

▲▶ **The longbow** was the weapon of the English, whose archers first started to practice bending the wooden bows when they were children. The bows were 1.8m (6ft) long and fired one-metre-long (3ft) arrows, with metal tips that could pierce armour at a range of 180m (600ft). A trained bowman could fire up to 12 arrows a minute. After firing a volley, the archers used to run forward and refill their quivers with arrows pulled from the dead and dying.

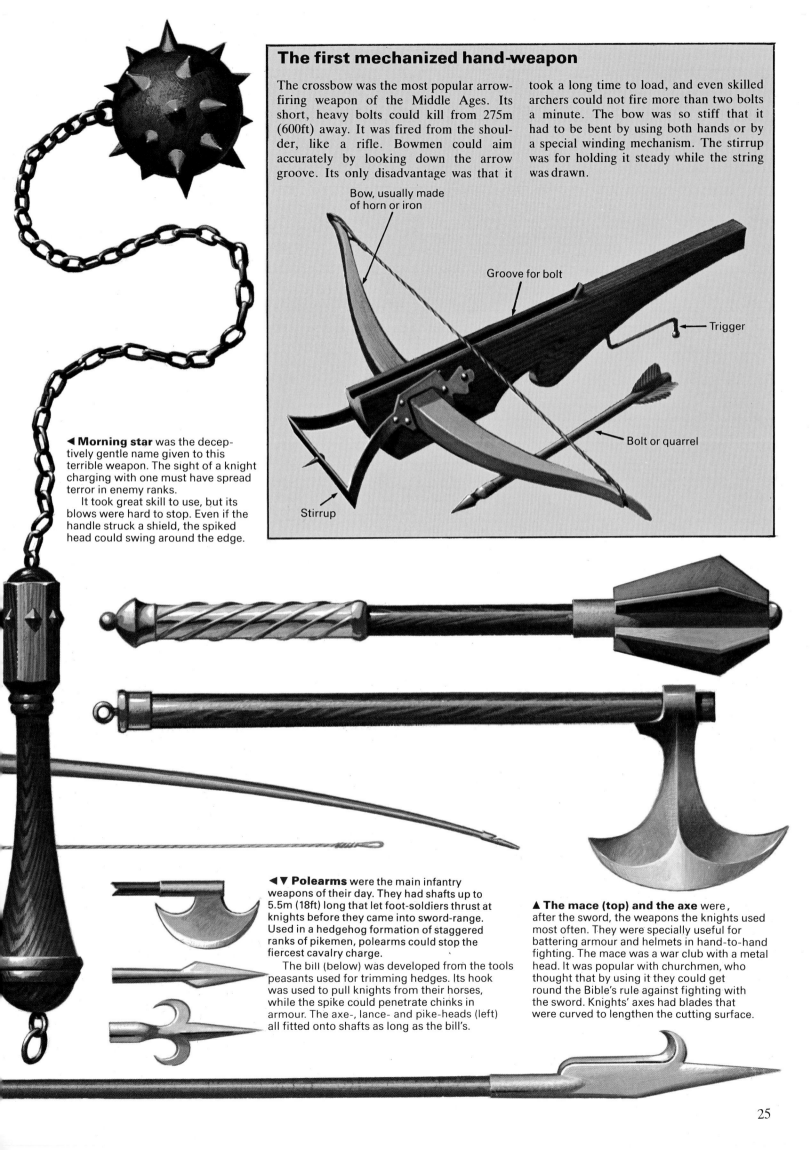

The first mechanized hand-weapon

The crossbow was the most popular arrow-firing weapon of the Middle Ages. Its short, heavy bolts could kill from 275m (600ft) away. It was fired from the shoulder, like a rifle. Bowmen could aim accurately by looking down the arrow groove. Its only disadvantage was that it took a long time to load, and even skilled archers could not fire more than two bolts a minute. The bow was so stiff that it had to be bent by using both hands or by a special winding mechanism. The stirrup was for holding it steady while the string was drawn.

Bow, usually made of horn or iron

Groove for bolt

Trigger

Bolt or quarrel

Stirrup

◄ **Morning star** was the deceptively gentle name given to this terrible weapon. The sight of a knight charging with one must have spread terror in enemy ranks.

It took great skill to use, but its blows were hard to stop. Even if the handle struck a shield, the spiked head could swing around the edge.

◄▼ **Polearms** were the main infantry weapons of their day. They had shafts up to 5.5m (18ft) long that let foot-soldiers thrust at knights before they came into sword-range. Used in a hedgehog formation of staggered ranks of pikemen, polearms could stop the fiercest cavalry charge.

The bill (below) was developed from the tools peasants used for trimming hedges. Its hook was used to pull knights from their horses, while the spike could penetrate chinks in armour. The axe-, lance- and pike-heads (left) all fitted onto shafts as long as the bill's.

▲ **The mace (top) and the axe** were, after the sword, the weapons the knights used most often. They were specially useful for battering armour and helmets in hand-to-hand fighting. The mace was a war club with a metal head. It was popular with churchmen, who thought that by using it they could get round the Bible's rule against fighting with the sword. Knights' axes had blades that were curved to lengthen the cutting surface.

CHIVALRY AND TOURNAMENTS

'Chivalry' comes from *chevalier*, the French word for a knight. It means the way a knight behaved, or rather the way he wanted to behave. He did not always live up to the ideals of chivalry.

Many of these ideals came from the Franks and other Germanic tribes. They were not very different from the ideals that soldiers always seem to have had. A knight was expected to be brave and fair. He was not supposed to kill anyone who had no chance of escaping. He was expected to be loyal to his friends, his lord and his king.

The knightly code of honour
The code of chivalry was rather vague until the time of the Crusades. Then the Church gave its blessing to knights who went on crusade. The knights began to put God into their feudal system, as the supreme lord. They made the same sort of promises to God as they did to their feudal lord.

Many of the crusaders came from the south and south-west of France. It was they who made up most of the rules of chivalry and the stories and songs and poems about it. They told about knights, the brave deeds they did and the women they loved.

Knights of other countries told stories too. These were often about their fore-fathers and other heroes in their history.

Heroes of chivalry
The German knights told stories about Siegfried and the Nibelungs. They were originally Burgundians, a Germanic tribe who settled in eastern France. The Germans also told stories about Theodoric the Ostrogoth, whom they called Dietrich von Bern, and Attila the Hun, whom they called Etzel.

English knights liked tales about King Arthur. French knights told stories about Charlemagne. They were all about bravery in battle, loyalty, treachery and love.

It took a long time and a lot of training for a man to become a knight. He had to be fit in every way, in mind and body. A young man of noble family first spent many years as squire to a knight – sometimes to his father or another near relation. He served the knight both on and off the battlefield. If he fought well, he might be knighted on the battlefield by the king or the commander.

A lot of money had to be spent when a man became a knight. So the son of a poor knight often had to wait a long time. He

had to have a horse, armour and weapons. There was feasting, and perhaps a tournament in which the new knight would show off his skill.

Tournaments were the favourite sport of knights, and were also good training for war. They first became popular at the time of the First Crusade.

Early tournaments were very like real battles. They were fought with sharp weapons over large areas, and knights were often killed.

Because of this the leaders of the Church tried to stop tournaments. And some kings of England would only let them be held by their permission. They were afraid that when the knights met they would plot against the government.

In about 1300 new rules were made for tournaments. Now only blunt weapons could be used. And a knight could have only three squires with him. Anyone who broke the rules was put in prison.

Jousting – war as sport
A new and less dangerous way of fighting also became popular. This was the joust. Knights charged at each other with lances. But the lances were made so that they broke easily when they hit the

▶ **Tournaments were splendid affairs.** There was dancing and feasting every evening, and all day long on Fridays, Saturdays and Sundays, when jousting was banned by the Church. The knights chose whether to fight with real or blunted weapons. They risked losing their ladies' esteem if they were defeated, as well as their horses and armour.

▼ **Squires practised jousting** against quintains – revolving targets set on poles. At the far end of the crosspiece was a bag filled with water or sand. If the squire failed to follow through fast enough, the bag would hit him as it swung round, sometimes hard enough to knock him off his horse.

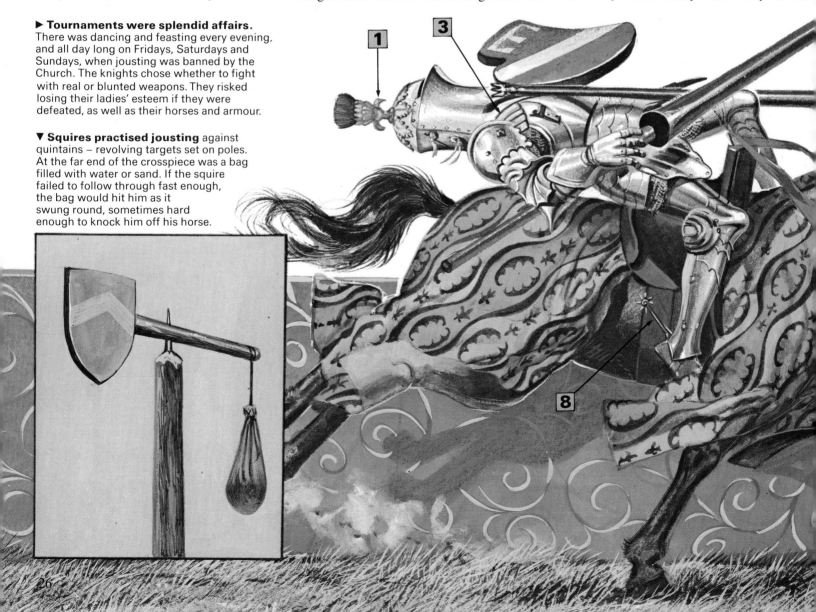

knight or his shield. Points were scored for hitting various parts of the body.

Special armour was used in tournaments. It was heavier and more decorative than the armour used in battle.

Ceremonies of the lists

The ceremonies that went with the tournament became more and more important. The fighting itself became less important and very formal. The special armour protected the body well. There were fewer accidents, though knights were still sometimes badly hurt, and even killed.

The large area set aside for the jousting was called the lists. A wooden barrier, called the tilt, went down the middle. This stopped horses from crashing into each other.

Spectators sat in special stands. All round there would be gaily coloured pavilions – luxurious tents where the knights put on their armour.

Tournaments were very colourful. They were still popular for about a hundred years after the knight stopped playing an important part on the battlefield.

Another way of proving courage was the *pas d'armes*. A band of knights would undertake to hold a given place against all comers, in honour of their ladies. At Orbigo in Spain in 1434, ten knights held a bridge against 68 challengers for a month, fighting more than 700 jousts.

▲ **The fiercest part of a tournament** was the melée. Teams of knights fought one another in the hope of taking captives to exchange for ransoms. In early tournaments, these fights often turned into real battles.

Equipment for the lists

1 **Elaborate crests** helped to identify the knights. Rivals could score points by knocking them off.

2 **Shields** were the normal targets for jousters. They aimed at the nails that fastened the arm-grip.

3 **Throat armour** was another common target. if it was faultily made, a blow here could be fatal.

4 **Lances** were made to shatter easily. After breaking three of them, the knights dismounted to fight on foot.

5 **The coronal** – a pronged lancehead shaped like a crown – was less dangerous than a sharp point.

6 **The raised cantle** at the back of the saddle made it difficult to unhorse knights.

7 **The tilt** prevented the horses from colliding. Knights jousting over it often missed each other completely.

8 **Spurs.** To have these cut off was a mark of dishonour.

9 **Horse armour.** Not much of this was needed when fighting at the tilt. To strike a horse with the lance meant disqualification from the tournament.

10 **Tilt armour** became more and more elaborate over the years. It was finally so complicated and heavy that the horses could barely manage to trot.

INDEX